Journal
of
Romanian Studies

Vol. 3, No. 1 (2021)

JRS editors
Peter Gross and Svetlana Suveica

JRS review editor
Iuliu Rațiu

JRS Editorial Assistant
Claudia Lonkin

About the Society for Romanian Studies

THE SOCIETY FOR ROMANIAN STUDIES (SRS) *is an international interdisciplinary academic organization founded in 1973 and dedicated to promoting research and critical studies on all aspects of Romanian and Moldovan culture and society. The SRS is recognized as the major North American professional organization for scholars concerned with Romania, Moldova, and their diasporas.*

SRS is affiliated with the South East European Studies Association (SEESA); the Association for Slavic, East European and Eurasian Studies (ASEEES—formerly known as the American Association for the Advancement of Slavic Studies or AAASS); the American Political Science Association (APSA); the American Historical Association (AHA); and the Romanian Studies Association of America (RSAA).

SRS offers a number of programs and activities to its members, including the peer-reviewed *Journal of Romanian Studies*, a biannual newsletter, the Romanian Studies book series published in collaboration with the publishing house Polirom in Iași, a mentoring program, prizes for exceptional scholarship in two different categories, as well as an international conference organized every three years in Romania.

More information about the SRS, including current officers, the national board, and membership information, can be found on the SRS website at *https://society4romanianstudies.org*.

www.society4romanianstudies.org
The Society for Romanian Studies

Editorial Board:

PETER GROSS (pgross@utk.edu) and
SVETLANA SUVEICA (ssuveica@gmail.com)
JRS editors

IULIU RAȚIU (bookreviewsjrs@gmail.com)
JRS review editor

CLAUDIA LONKIN (claudia.lonkin@gmail.com)
JRS Editorial Assistant

Advisory Board:

DENNIS DELETANT (Georgetown University, USA)
JON FOX (University of Bristol, UK)
VALENTINA GLAJAR (Texas State University, USA)
PETER GROSS (University of Tennessee, USA)
BRIGID HAINES (Swansea University, UK)
IRINA LIVEZEANU (University of Pittsburgh, USA)
MIHAELA MIROIU (National School of Political Science and Public Administration, Romania)
STEVE D. ROPER (Florida Atlantic University, USA)
DOMNICA RADULESCU (Washington and Lee University, USA)
PAUL E. SUM (University of North Dakota, USA)
CRISTIAN TILEAGA (Loughborough University, UK)
VLADIMIR TISMANEANU (University of Maryland, College Park, USA)
LUCIAN TURCESCU (Concordia University, Montreal, Canada)

Bibliographic information published by the Deutsche Nationalbibliothek
The Deutsche Nationalbibliothek lists this publication in the Deutsche Nationalbibliografie; detailed bibliographic data are available on the Internet at http://dnb.dnb.de.

Bibliografische Information der Deutschen Nationalbibliothek
Die Deutsche Nationalbibliothek verzeichnet diese Publikation in der Deutschen Nationalbibliografie; detaillierte bibliografische Daten sind im Internet über http://dnb.d-nb.de abrufbar.

Journal of Romanian Studies
Vol. 3, No. 1 (2021)

Stuttgart: *ibidem*-Verlag / *ibidem* Press

Erscheinungsweise: halbjährlich / Frequency: biannual

ISBN 978-3-8382-1569-3

ISSN 2627-5325

Ordering Information:
PRINT: Subscription (two copies per year): € 58.00 / year (+ S&H: € 6.00 / year within Germany, € 10.00 / year international). The subscription can be canceled at any time.
Single copy or back issue: € 34.00 / copy (+ S&H: € 3.00 within Germany, € 4.50 international).

E-BOOK: Subscription (two copies per year): € 35.99 / year, individual copy or back issue: € 24.99 / copy. Available via ibidem.eu.

For further information please visit www.ibidem.eu/jrs.htm

© *ibidem*-Verlag / *ibidem* Press
Stuttgart, Germany 2021

Alle Rechte vorbehalten
Das Werk einschließlich aller seiner Teile ist urheberrechtlich geschützt. Jede Verwertung außerhalb der engen Grenzen des Urheberrechtsgesetzes ist ohne Zustimmung des Verlages unzulässig und strafbar. Dies gilt insbesondere für Vervielfältigungen, Übersetzungen, Mikroverfilmungen und elektronische Speicherformen sowie die Einspeicherung und Verarbeitung in elektronischen Systemen.

All rights reserved

No part of this publication may be reproduced, stored in or introduced into a retrieval system, or transmitted, in any form, or by any means (electronical, mechanical, photocopying, recording or otherwise) without the prior written permission of the publisher.
Any person who performs any unauthorized act in relation to this publication may be liable to criminal prosecution and civil claims for damages.

Printed in the EU

Contents

Note from the Editors
 Peter Gross, Iuliu Rațiu and Claudia Lonkin 7

Obituary: Keith Hitchins (1931–2020)
 Dennis Deletant 9

ARTICLES

The Shape of Interwar Romanian History
 Roland Clark 11

The Romanian Orthodox Church and its Financial Dealings in Post-Communism
 Lavinia Stan and Lucian Turcescu 43

Shaping, Questioning, Contradicting "Bad Communism:" Aspects of Generational Memory in Romania after 1989
 Valeska Bopp-Filimonov 65

Re-Envisioning Cubism in Romanian Avant-Garde Magazines
 Amelia Miholca 85

The Romanian Judicial Professions Database: An Open-Source Tool for Researching the Romanian Legal System
 Radu Pârvulescu 113

REVIEWS

Constantin Iordachi. Liberalism, Constitutional Nationalism, and Minorities: The Making of Romanian Citizenship, c. 1750–1918.
  Review by Mara Mărginean 121

Sabrina P. Ramet. Interwar East Central Europe, 1918–1941: The Failure of Democracy-building, the Fate of Minorities.
  Review by Francesco Magno 125

Dorina Roșca. Le grand tournant de la société moldave. "Intellectuels" et capital social dans la transformation post-socialiste.
  Review by Petru Negură 127

Contributors 131

Note from the Editors

We regret losing Dr. Diane Vancea as our co-editor and want to thank her for her contribution to the JRS in the short months she was a leading member of our team. We congratulate her on her election as President of Ovidius University's (Constanța, Romania) faculty senate, the very reason her schedule will no longer allow her to serve with us.

We are fortunate to have identified a great successor for Dr. Vancea. Please join us in welcoming a new co-editor, Dr. Svetlana Suveica.

Image source: IOS/neverflash.com

She is a Research fellow at the Leibniz-Institute for East and Southeast European Studies (IOS) in Regensburg, Germany. Her research specialty centers on East- and Southeast European History (with focus on Romania, Moldova and Ukraine); World War I and post-war transformations; World War II; Holocaust in Southeastern Europe; socio-political transformations in post-communist East European societies.

Co-Editor, Peter Gross
Book Review Editor, Iuliu Rațiu
Editorial Assistant, Claudia Lonkin

Keith Hitchins (1931–2020)

My contact with Keith dates from the publication in 1969 of his groundbreaking *The Rumanian National Movement in Transylvania, 1780–1849.* For a newly-appointed teacher of early Romanian literature at the School of Slavonic and East European Studies at the University of London, the book proved invaluable. It represented an example of outstanding scholarship, delivered with the detachment of a foreigner from national and confessional prejudices. I expressed these sentiments in a letter that I wrote to him and received gracious thanks. The same qualities characterized his study *Orthodoxy and Nationality: Andreiu Şaguna and the Rumanians of Transylvania, 1846–1873,* that appeared in 1977. Once again, I was indebted to Keith, since my teaching obligations were extended to cover the history of Romania in the following year. Şaguna was not only the central figure in the national movement in the two decades after the 1848 revolution, but was also extraordinarily active as an Orthodox prelate, as a theologian, and in organizing education. The exchange of occasional letters paved the way to our first meeting, in autumn 1988, in Cluj, in the office of Pompiliu Teodor, Professor of History at Babeş-Bolyai University.

Our shared dismay at the draconian austerity measures imposed by Ceauşescu on the long-suffering Romanian people translated our relationship into one of friendship, a friendship that was renewed after 1989 when our association revolved around Şerban Papacostea in Bucharest. Perhaps fittingly, Şerban provided the opportunity for Keith and I to discuss our respective projects on a number of occasions. Taking advantage of our fortuitous presence in the capital, he invited us both either for morning coffee and cakes in his study, or for an afternoon version, in which the cakes were supplemented by fruit salad, and the coffee by Romanian vermouth.

Keith's major project in the early 1990s was a monumental history of Romania, spanning the years 1774 to 1947. The typescript proved to be so voluminous that Sir William Deakin, who, alongside Alan Bullock, was one the editors of *The Oxford History of Modern Europe,* in which series Keith's contribution was contracted to appear, became concerned and asked me to cast an eye over it. I and a second consultant suggested that the typescript be divided into two volumes and indeed it appeared as *Rumania, 1866–1947* (1994) and *The Romanians, 1774–1866* (1996). Unique in the English-language cannon and meticulously researched, both books are a testament to Keith's almost monastic devotion to his *métier*, and stand as valuable works of reference.

Șerban's study also provided the crucible for *Istoria României*, a 600-page volume published by Editura Enciclopedică in 1998. Șerban himself initiated the project and invited Keith and I to join him, alongside Mihai Bărbulescu and Pompiliu Teodor, as authors. The book was revised and reprinted in several editions over the next five years by Editura Corint. Keith, Șerban and I discussed the revisions to our own chapters and took much pleasure in the positive feedback that we received from Romanian students who informed us that in several universities it had been adopted as a core coursebook. It was in this setting that Keith's personal qualities were also displayed: his interest in his graduate and postgraduate students, his altruism, his objectivity, and his humility. He was an admirable example of a dedicated scholar and teacher.

Dennis Deletant OBE
Emeritus Professor, School of Slavonic and East European Studies,
University College, London
Visiting Ion Rațiu Professor of Romanian Studies,
Georgetown University, Washington DC (2011–2020)

Articles

The Shape of Interwar Romanian History

Roland Clark

Abstract: *This article reviews some of the major frameworks that historians use to tell the stories of interwar Romania, asking why they became popular and how useful they are in the twenty-first century. It examines the problems of periodization and the placement of the nation-state at the center of Romanian history, then traces the evolution of four major framing narratives: (1) the problems of a small state; (2) the collapse of democracy; (3) the march of progress; and (4) the consequences of state-building and centralization. Such approaches give the impression that interwar Romania was an intolerant, chauvinistic society that marginalized anyone who was not male, Orthodox, and ethnically Romanian. The best new histories, however, not only uncover alternative, suppressed narratives but also reveal how people were able to live and sometimes thrive in a society as diverse as interwar Romania undeniably was.*

How does one tell the story of what happened in Greater Romania between the two world wars? Was it "a time like no other" (*odată ca niciodată*), as in the fables, or did it share continuities, institutions, identities, and discourses with other stories from different eras? When does the story begin and end? Who are its main characters and who was simply there as background? What are the important themes that attentive readers of history books should take away with them? In Penelope Corfield's terms, how does "continuity (or persistence)", fit with "micro-change (or momentum) and macro-change (or turbulence)"?[1] No single framework can encapsulate the rich messiness of reality, but historians choose whichever frames help them make sense of the past most clearly. As the German historian Ulrich Herbert has pointed out, various historians have framed the story of twentieth century Europe as one of the conflict between the bourgeoisie and the working classes, of the creation of the West and the German *Sonderweg*, of a battle between liberalism, fascism, and

---

1   Penelope J. Corfield, *Time and the Shape of History* (New Haven: Yale University Press, 2007), 212.

communism, or of the climax and passing of high modernity.[2] This article reviews some of the major frameworks that historians use to tell the stories of interwar Romania, asking why they became popular and how useful they are in the twenty-first century. Jean-François Lyotard has famously argued that in the postmodern world we no longer rely on a handful of "grand narratives," but on multiple small narratives.[3] Yet as I argue below, most historians of Romania continue to use many of the same broad, overarching frameworks that historical actors themselves used to make sense of their world.

All frameworks privilege some traces of the past over others, marginalizing certain stories through omission. They also reflect the interests and mental maps of those social groups they were created for.[4] Before we reproduce these we need to ask whose purposes they serve, whom they empower, and whom they exclude. Moreover, in the same way that the scientific paradigms discussed by Thomas Kuhn shift when new evidence suggests that older paradigms do not describe reality well enough, frameworks are only useful insofar as they explain the evidence that we have available.[5] Has the unprecedented access to national archives and the archives of the Securitate that we have had over the past twenty years produced new narratives and/or invalidated old ones? To what extent is the way we talk about interwar Romania shaped by the questions of the twenty-first century? These questions do not attempt to discredit particular frameworks, merely to emphasize their contingency, assess their usefulness and limitations, and provoke new ways of looking at evidence.

After discussing the problems of periodization and of placing the nation-state at the center of Romanian history, I trace the evolution of four major frames that continue to shape how historians think about interwar Romania: (1) the problems of a small state; (2) the collapse of democracy; (3) the march of progress; and (4) the consequences of state-building and

---

2   Ulrich Herbert, "Europe in High Modernity: Reflections on a Theory of the 20th Century," *Journal of Modern European History*, 5, no. 1 (2007): 5–21.
3   Jean-François Lyotard, *The Postmodern Condition: A Report on Knowledge*, transl. Geoff Bennington and Brian Massumi (Minneapolis: University of Minnesota Press, 1984).
4   Balázs Trencsényi, Marja Jalava, and Diana Mishkova (eds), "Regimes of Historicity" in *Southeastern and Northern Europe, 1890–1945: Discourses of Identity and Temporality* (Basingstoke: Palgrave Macmillan, 2014); Christopher Clark, *Time and Power: Visions of History in German Politics, from the Thirty Years' War to the Third Reich* (Princeton: Princeton University Press, 2019).
5   Thomas Kuhn, *The Structure of Scientific Revolutions* (Chicago: University of Chicago Press, 1970).

centralization. Such approaches give the impression that interwar Romania was an intolerant, chauvinistic society that marginalized anyone who was not male, Orthodox, and ethnically Romanian. As I argue in the final section, however, the best new histories are those which not only uncover alternative, suppressed narratives but also reveal how people were able to live and sometimes thrive in a society as diverse as interwar Romania undeniably was.

Periodization

It is difficult to challenge the idea that there *was* an interwar period. Many Romanians experienced the end of the First World War and the defeat of Béla Kun's Hungary as a watershed moment that set the stage for greatly expanded borders, a decisively pro-French, pro-League of Nations foreign policy, universal male suffrage, the reconfiguration of the major political alliances, new labor laws, land redistribution, and rapid urbanization and industrialization. In the words of Nicolae Iorga, in 1918 contemporaries hoped that "a new Romania, a courageous and pure country must emerge from our sufferings."[6] Twenty years later, the establishment of Carol II's royal dictatorship in February 1938 meant the end of parliamentary government and a geopolitical shift towards foreign and economic policies oriented towards Germany, as well as a major shift in how individuals related to one another and to the state. Media censorship intensified significantly, the brutal repression of the Legion of the Archangel Michael emphasized how serious the king was about banning political parties, and the National Renaissance Front's influence in schools and the civil service established a single party as the locus of social and political power. Carol II's regime curtailed the civil rights of most Romanian citizens, but none more so than Romanian Jews, who were barred from working in public institutions and in certain industries, had their newspapers banned, and lost jobs, businesses, and eventually their citizenship.[7] Finally, the territorial gains which defined Greater Romania were spectacularly reversed with the loss of Bessarabia and Northern Bukovina to the Soviet Union in June 1940, Northern Transylvania to Hungary in August, and Southern Dobruja to Bulgaria in September. By the time the National Legionary

---

6   Comitetul de conducere, "Chemare," *Neamul românesc*, 13, no. 353 (23 December 1918): 1.
7   Philippe Henri Blasen, *La "primauté de la nation roumaine" et les "étrangers": Les minorités et leur liberté du travail sous le cabinet Goga et la dictature royale (décembre 1937–septembre 1940)* (PhD dissertation, Universitatea Babeș-Bolyai, Cluj-Napoca, 2020).

State was established in September 1940, the constellation of economic, social, cultural, and political conditions that most historians associate with the interwar period were well and truly history.

Treating the interwar period as a coherent whole has certain advantages. It emphasizes ruptures with the past and the future and stresses the synchronic over the diachronic. Periodization reveals flows and influences that we might otherwise not have noticed. Subsequently, it encourages historians to look for the underlying myths or narratives—what Fredric Jameson calls the "political unconscious"—that contemporaries believed gave meaning to their world.[8] Only by telling stories that have a beginning, a middle, and an end can we begin to get at the evolution of historical phenomena.

Talking about an "interwar period" is nonetheless problematic because it obscures the continuities between pre-war, wartime, and post-war societies. Significant continuities do exist, particularly in terms of the centrality of what Katherine Verdery calls "national ideology" to Romanian discourses.[9] Institutional continuities also existed. One cannot understand the Securitate, for example, without understanding what it inherited from its interwar predecessor, the Siguranță.[10] Historians often mention continuities between institutions and laws in the Old Kingdom and those of Greater Romania, but remarkably little attention has been paid to continuities between Hungarian, Austrian, and Russian legacies and interwar Romania. Paul Brunsanowski's research on the unification of the Romanian Orthodox Church during the 1920s and Francesco Magno's work on regionalism in the legal system shows that imperial legacies had a significant impact on the shape of the interwar nation-state.[11] It is likely that similar continuities could be found in most regional institutions.

---

8   Fredric Jameson, *The Political Unconscious: Narrative as a Socially Symbolic Act* (London: Routledge, 2010), 12–3, 102.

9   Katherine Verdery, *National Ideology Under Socialism: Identity and Cultural Politics in Ceaușescu's Romania* (Berkeley: University of California Press, 1991).

10   Alin Spânu, *Istoria serviciilor de informații/contrainformații românești în perioada 1919–1945* (Iași: Demiurg), 201.

11   Paul Brunsanowski, *Reforma constituțională din Biserica Ortodoxă a Transilvaniei între 1850–1925* (Cluj-Napoca: Presa Universitară Clujeană, 2007); Paul Brunsanowski, *Autonomia și constituționalismul în dezbaterile privind unificarea Bisericii Ortodoxe Române (1919–1925)* (Cluj-Napoca: Presa Universitară Clujeană, 2007). Cf. Francesco Magno, *Law and Justice in Interwar Romania. National, Regional and Professional Identities* (PhD dissertation, University of Trento, 2020).

Tracing individual biographies is one effective way to transcend the interwar/postwar binary by revealing continuities within and across historical ruptures. Robert Levy's biography of Ana Pauker, for example, demonstrates that beyond the before-and-after-1944 story of the Romanian Communist Party lie other stories about the status of Jews and women. As Levy argues, Pauker's dual "otherness" as both a Jew and a woman shaped her political decisions *throughout* her life, not just once she came to power.[12] By and large, however, Pauker's story was the exception rather than the rule. In Luciana Jinga's words, by the end of the interwar period the influence of female communist activists had been roundly defeated: "If they stayed alive they found themselves marginalized and only a few were able to return to prominence within the party."[13]

Prosopographical studies of intellectuals in particular have helped explain how individuals and institutions navigated ruptures such as the two world wars and the rise of state socialism.[14] The research collected in Cristian Vasile's *"We Need People"* (2017) focuses on "mechanisms of change" during transitional periods, showing how elites who had pursued successful careers as fascists during the 1930s managed to salvage their professional status after the war by "retreating into a strictly specialized area."[15] Individuals who had struggled professionally during the interwar period because of their left-wing sympathies flourished after the war.[16] Far from being a decisive break after 23 August 1944, personal alliances and modus operandi established during the 1930s continued to shape careers and institutional practices well into the 1970s.[17] Acknowledging continuities is not to deny the significance of periodization. Rather, the challenge is to show how old institutions, ideas, and individuals adapted to new contexts.

---

12 Robert Levy, *Ana Pauker: The Rise and Fall of a Jewish Communist* (Berkeley: University of California Press, 2001).
13 Luciana M. Jinga, *Gen și reprezentare în România comunistă 1944–1989* (Iași: Polirom, 2015), 59.
14 Lucian Nastasă, *Intelectualii și promovarea socială (Pentru o morfologie a câmpului universitar)* (Cluj: Editura Nereamia Napocae, 2003); Lucian Boia, *Capcanele istoriei: Elita intelectuală românească între 1930 și 1950* (București: Humanitas, 2011).
15 Valentin Săndulescu, "Convertiri și reconvertiri: elite academice și culturale și schmibare politcă în România anilor 1930–1960," in *"Ne trebuie oameni!": Elite intelectuale și transformări istorice în România modernă și contemporană*, ed. Cristian Vasile (Târgoviște: Editura Cetatea de Scaun, 2017), 141–80.
16 Camelia Zavarache, "Geometria unei relații complexe: elite, modele ale modernizării statale și regimuri politice în România secolului XX," in *"Ne trebuie oameni!"*, 181–283.
17 Anca Șincan, "Portretul lui N. Despărțirea de ortodoxia comunistă: despre politica religioasă după 1948," in *"Ne trebuie oameni!"*, 317–36.

The Nation-State

In the vast majority of histories the Romanian nation-state functions as the central protagonist. As did most historians of the nineteenth century, Alexandru D. Xenopol and Nicolae Iorga placed the nation at the center of their major synthetic histories. They defined it in cultural and linguistic terms and treated it as an historical actor that emerged in Roman Dacia during the second century.[18] Constantin C. Giurescu and R. W. Seton-Watson echoed their approach and after a lull of several decades, frames emphasizing Romanian national specificity continued under state socialism during the 1970s and 1980s.[19] A great deal of nuance and clarification is needed if the nationalist narrative is to have any value. Balázs Trencsényi and others have shown that national identities were created for specific political goals and instrumentalized in an unprecedented way during the interwar period, but most historians continue to adopt "Romanian" as an unproblematic category and reify it through constant use.[20]

The fragility of Romanian-ness becomes apparent when one looks at people who had to struggle to be recognized as Romanians. Although a host of early twentieth century writers had emphasized the Romanian national identity of Aromanians living in northern Macedonia, when these people migrated to Romania during the 1920s they were not accorded the same "ethnic privileges" as their co-nationals.[21] In Moldavia, the Romanian state maintained an ambiguous attitude towards the Hungarian-speaking Csángós the threat of deportation during the Second World War prompted them into attempting to prove their Romanianness.[22] Nor were

---

18   Alexandru D. Xenopol, *Histoire des Roumains de la Dacie Trajane: depuis les origines jusqu'a l'union des principautés en 1859* (Paris: Leroux, 1896), 110; Nicolae Iorga, *Istoria românilor*, vol. 1.2 (București: s.n., 1936).

19   Constantin C. Giurescu, *Istoria românilor*, 2nd edition (București: Fundația Regală pentru Literatură și Artă, 1935); Robert William Seton-Watson, *A History of the Roumanians: From the Roman Times to the Completion of Unity* (Cambridge: Cambridge University Press, 1934); Dennis Deletant, "Re-Writing the Past: Trends in Contemporary Romanian Historiography," in Dennis Deletant and Maurice Pearton, *Romania Observed: Studies in Contemporary Romanian History* (Bucharest: Encyclopaedic Publishing House, 1998), 276–303; Lucian Boia, *History and Myth in Romanian Consciousness*, transl. James Christian Brown (Budapest: Central European University Press, 2001), 70–82.

20   Balázs Trencsényi, *The Politics of National Character: A Study in Interwar East European Thought* (London: Routledge, 2013).

21   Roland Clark, "Claiming Ethnic Privilege: Aromanian Immigrants and Romanian Fascist Politics," *Contemporary European History*, 24, no. 1 (2015): 37–49.

22   R. Chris Davis, *Hungarian Religion, Romanian Blood: A Minority's Struggle for National Belonging, 1920–1945* (Madison, WI: University of Wisconsin Press, 2018).

all territories included in Greater Romania obviously "Romanian." Romanian elites considered northern Dobruja to be an Ottoman borderland when they annexed it in 1878. Far from identifying its inhabitants as Romanians, opponents of annexation claimed that these people were "an assemblage of the most turbulent elements, gathered there from all over the world."[23] Romania's leaders did consider Transylvania to be Romanian, but that region's national identity was far from being a foregone conclusion in the interwar period.[24] As Lucian Boia points out, in 1910 only 53.8 percent of Transylvanians were Romanian speakers, 31.6 percent spoke Hungarian, and 10.7 percent German, and the status of the territory continued to be contested until the end of the Second World War.[25]

National labels become particularly problematic when applied to minorities. When historians refer to "Romanians", for example, are they also talking about Jews, Muslims, or Roma? These people were citizens of the nation-state but outsiders in other ways.[26] Their articulation as outsiders was crucial for defining Romanians as a dominant group and historians reinforce the insider-outside binary whenever they fail to challenge it.[27] Historians need to be deliberate about which aspects of historical identity are being highlighted by their labels. The term "Romanian Jews" is no more ideologically neutral than "Jewish Romanians," but historians have consistently chosen the former term, which satisfies both Jewish nationalism's desire to identify people as ethnically Jewish regardless of their country of origin and Romanian nationalism's desire to exclude them from the nation. Talking about "Romanian Jews" also masks cleavages within the Jewish community, which recognized differences between "Hungarian Jews" and "Saxon Jews" based on whether their families came from Transylvania or Bukovina and whether they were more comfortable speaking Hungarian or German. Structuring Romanian history around national identities also ignores the multiple instances of national indifference and solidarities across religious and ethnic boundaries that have

---

23 Quoted in Constantin Iordachi, *Citizenship, Nation- and State-Building: The Integration of Northern Dobrogea into Romania, 1878–1913* (Pittsburgh: University of Pittsburgh Press, 2002), 12.
24 Rogers Brubaker, Margit Feischmidt, Jon Fox, and Liana Grancea, *Nationalist Politics and Everyday Ethnicity in a Transylvanian Town* (Princeton: Princeton University Press, 2006), 97–101; Holly Case, *Between States: The Transylvanian Question and the European Idea during World War II* (Stanford: Stanford University Press, 2009).
25 Lucian Boia, *Cum s-a românizat România* (București: Humanitas, 2015), 45.
26 Carol Iancu, *Evreii din România, 1919–1938. De la emancipare la marginalizare* (Bucharest: Hasefer, 2000).
27 Shannon Woodcock, *The Țigan Is Not a Man: The Țigan Other as Catalyst for Romanian Ethnonational Identity* (PhD dissertation, University of Sydney, 2005), 6.

been highlighted by historians of places elsewhere in Eastern Europe but are largely ignored by historians of Romania.[28] The volume *Identities In-Between in East-Central Europe* (2019) helpfully moves beyond nationality to look at "subcultures", emphasizing temporary identities and intersectionality in a rethinking of categories of analysis that bodes well for the future of the field.[29]

People who did not interact with the state and/or who did not identify as Romanian are almost invisible in interwar archives except when they had to apply for special permits to hold cultural or religious celebrations. As Sorin Radu and Oliver Jens Schmitt point out, we know remarkably little about interactions between elites and peasants apart from in the context of the Gusti School's monographic projects.[30] The silence of non-elite actors fuels the perception that there were in fact two Romanias—one of the educated urban elites and one of the rural poor.[31] Such interpretations are, of course, undermined by the wealth of documentation detailing sustained interactions between cities and the countryside throughout the period.

Women are also marginalized, both in the archival records and by historians, many of whom write as if no women lived in interwar Romania. Historians of feminism have noted the limited civil rights enjoyed by women in early twentieth century Romania, the determined opposition feminists faced at all levels of society, and the limitations of their success in legal and economic terms.[32] By focusing exclusively on feminist politics, however, most ignore the key role that industrialization, urbanization,

---

28 István Deák, *Beyond Nationalism: A Social and Political History of the Habsburg Officer Corps, 1848–1918* (New York: Oxford University Press, 2010); Emily Greble, *Sarajevo, 1941–1945: Muslims, Christians, and Jews in Hitler's Europe* (Ithaca: Cornell University Press, 2011).
29 Jan Fellerer, Robert Pyrah, and Marius Turda (eds), *Identities In-Between in East-Central Europe* (London: Routledge, 2019).
30 Sorin Radu and Oliver Jens Schmitt, 'Introduction', in *Politics and Peasants in Interwar Romania: Perceptions, Mentalities, Propaganda*, eds. Oliver Jens Schmitt and Sorin Radu (Newcastle upon Tyne: Cambridge Scholars Publishing, 2017), 1–24.
31 Ionuț Butoi, *Mircea Vulcănescu: O microistorie a interbelicului românesc* (București: Eikon, 2015), 15–45.
32 Paraschiva Câncea, *Mișcarea pentru emanciparea femeii în România: 1848–1948* (București: Editura Politică, 1976); Ghizela Cosma, *Femeile și politica în România: Evoluția dreptului de vot în perioada interbelică* (Cluj-Napoca: Presa Universitară Clujeană, 2002); Ghizela Cosma and Virgiliu Țârău (eds), *Condiția femeii în România în secolul XX: Studii de caz* (Cluj-Napoca: Presa Universitară Clujeană, 2002); Mihaela Miroiu and Maria Bucur (eds), *Patriarhat și emancipare în istoria gândirii politice românești* (Bucharest: Editura Polirom, 2002); Maria Bucur and Mihaela Miroiu, *Birth of Democratic Citizenship: Women in Modern Romania* (Bloomington: Indiana University Press, 2018).

and the introduction of universal male suffrage had on women's roles. Moreover, those histories that focus exclusively on the early twentieth century implicitly frame the struggle as a teleological story connecting feminist activism in the past with rights enjoyed by women in the present, marginalizing the extraordinary impact of state socialism on Romanian women.[33] Paraschiva Câncea, Ghizela Cosma, Mihaela Miroiu, Maria Bucur and others have had little choice about focusing disproportionately on feminist activists to the exclusion of other women because until recently the story of Romanian feminism was almost unknown, and their work has been a necessary first step towards the full integration of women into the history of the interwar period.

Cristina Sircuța's *Women's Lives in Interwar Romania* (2017) is the first study that addresses the impact of broad social and political change on women's lives during this period. Women's history rather than gender history, it explores how women experienced the First World War, female education, women in the workforce, family life and changing attitudes towards women, women's contributions to the arts, literature, and theatre, women's involvement in right wing politics, women's leisure activities, fashion, and the feminist and anti-feminist movements. Sircuța thus opens up a wide variety of new research agendas that had hitherto been explored only in isolated journal articles or not at all. She notes that "we cannot talk of a single type of woman in the interwar period," but that the "different opportunities offered by life in the city or the countryside, and distinctions of wealth, income, and education" meant that women's lives differed radically from one another even while they shared common experiences of patriarchy and legal restrictions.[34] More focused research is needed on women from different walks of life, ages, and education. Gender histories of the interwar period are also sadly lacking, with the notable exception of Maria Bucur's seminal research and a handful of articles on women and fascism.[35] Zsuzsa Bokor and Ghizela Comsa have written

---

33　On the impact of state socialism on Romanian women, see Gail Kligman, *The Politics of Duplicity: Controlling Reproduction in Ceausescu's Romania* (Berkeley: University of California Press, 1998) and Jill Massino, *Ambiguous Transitions: Gender, the State, and Everyday Life in Socialist and Postsocialist Romania* (New York: Berghahn Books, 2019).

34　Cristina Sircuța, *Viața femeilor în România interbelică* (București: Oscar Print, 2017), 322.

35　Maria Bucur, "In Praise of Wellborn Mothers: On the Development of Eugenicist Gender Roles in Interwar Romania," *East European Politics and Societies,* 9, no. 1 (1995): 123–42; Maria Bucur, "Between the Mother of the Wounded and the Virgin of Jiu: Romanian Women and the Gender of Heroism during the Great War," *Journal of Women's History,* 12, no. 2 (2000): 30–56; Maria Bucur, "Gender and Fascism in

on the history of prostitution, and Cristina Bejan has discussed elite attitudes towards homosexuality, but their work stands almost alone on the shelf.[36] Of all the people ignored by the major frames of Romanian history, women are the most glaring omission, and their stories need to be integrated into future accounts of the period. The social and cultural contributions of ethnic minorities—Hungarians, Germans, Jews, Roma, Ukrainians and Poles—are also sadly missing from most histories, leaving us ignorant of their active involvement in Romanian society.[37]

The Problems of a "Small" State

A fervent supporter of independent nation-states as a means of maintaining the balance of power in Central Europe, the prominent historian R. W. Seton-Watson wrote in 1915 that "a hundred years ago Roumania consisted of two corrupt and backward vassal provinces of Turkey, without influence or consideration in the world. To-day she has been not unjustly described as 'the Belgium of the East,' progressing by leaps and bounds."[38]

Interwar Romania," in *Women, Gender and the Extreme Right in Europe* (Manchester: Manchester University Press, 2003), 58–79; Maria Bucur, "Romania," in *Women, Gender and Fascism in Europe, 1919–45* (New Brunswick, NJ: Rutgers Unviersity Press, 2003), 57–78; Roland Clark, "Die Damen der Legion: Frauen in rumäischen faschistischen Gruppierungen," transl. Andreas Rathberger, in *Inszenierte Gegenmacht von rechts: Die "Legion Erzengel Michael" in Rumänien 1918–1938*, eds. Armin Heinen and Oliver Jens Schmitt (München: Oldenbourg Verlag, 2013), 193–216; Mihai Stelian Rusu, "Domesticating Viragos. The Politics of Womanhood in the Romanian Legionary Movement," *Fascism*, 5, no. 2 (2016): 149–76.

36 Zsuzsa Bokor, *Testtörténetek. A nemzet és a nemi betegségek medikalizálása a két világháború közötti Kolozsváron* (Cluj-Napoca: Nemzeti Kisebbségkutató Intézet, 2013); Cristina A. Bejan, *Intellectuals and Fascism in Interwar Romania: The Criterion Association* (New York: Palgrave Macmillan, 2019), 177–209.

37 For example, Tudor Georgescu, *The Eugenic Fortress: The Transylvanian Saxon Experiment in Interwar Romania* (Budapest: Central European University Press, 2016); Margaret Beissinger, Speranța Rădulescu, and Anca Giurchescu (eds), *Manele in Romania: Cultural Expression and Social Meaning in Balkan Popular Music* (Lanham: Rowman and Littlefield, 2016); Ottmar Trașcă and Remus Gabriel Anghel (eds), *Un veac frământat: Germanii din România după 1918* (Cluj-Napoca: Institutul pentru Studierea Problemelor Minorităților Naționale, 2018); Anca Filipovici (ed), *Polonezii din România: repere identitare* (Cluj-Napoca: Institutul pentru Studierea Problemelor Minorităților Naționale, 2020).

38 R. W. Seton-Watson, *Roumania and the Great War* (London: Constable and Company, 1915), 2. On Seton-Watson's politics at the time, see László Péter, "R. W. Seton-Watson's Changing Views on the National Question of the Habsburg Monarchy and the European Balance of Power," *The Slavonic and East European Review*, 82, no. 3 (2004): 676–679. On his role in negotiations with Romania during 1915, see Hugh Seton-Watson and Christopher Seton-Watson, *The Making of a New Europe: R. W. Seton-Watson and the Last Years of Austria-Hungary* (London: Methuen, 1981), 114–5.

His account of Romanian history concluded that it was a small country which could easily influenced by the Great Powers, in particular, by Great Britain. In 1945, a survey of the interwar period written by his son, Hugh Seton-Watson, again characterized Eastern Europe as "a battle-ground of rival Imperialisms." He argued that the Eastern European countries "have shown themselves weak, divided and inexperienced," unable to solve their own problems. He told of "backward and apathetic" Romanian peasants ruled by vain and ambitious elites, concluding that "the future of Eastern Europe is inseparable from the future of the European Great Powers."[39] Other interwar accounts similarly emphasized the extent to which Great Power politics shaped Romanian political and economic realities, but pointed out that foreign intervention was a mixed blessing in Romania, as likely to harm the Great Powers' reputation as it was to help them.[40]

While acknowledging the undeniable impact of geopolitics, there has been an increasing trend for historians to emphasize Romanian agency and efforts to turn foreign ambitions to Romania's advantage.[41] Norman Stone's 1975 history of the Romania's involvement in the First World War argued that Romanian fortunes in the war were entirely dependent on what their French and Russian allies did or did not do, but more recent histories have revealed the extent to which decisions made by Romanians at all levels of society shaped the country's wartime experiences.[42]

Sherman David Spector's and Keith Hitchins' histories of the Paris Peace Conferences, for example, put Ion I. C. Brătianu in center stage. "In a sense," Hitchins writes, "Paris was the culmination of a grand strategy Brătianu had worked out in the preceding quarter-century to raise the

---

39 Hugh Seton-Watson, *Eastern Europe Between the Wars, 1918–1941* (Cambridge: Cambridge University Press, 1945), xiii, 213, 413.
40 Nicolae Iorga, Francis Bickley and Marion Newbigin, "Romania," in John Buchan (ed), *Bulgaria and Romania* (London: Hodder and Stoughton, 1924), 282–312; George Clenton Logio, *Rumania: Its History, Politics and Economics* (Manchester: Sherratt and Hughes, 1932).
41 For example, Valentin Naumescu (ed), *România, marile puteri şi ordinea europeană, 1918–2018* (Iaşi: Polirom, 2018); Svetlana Suveica (ed), *Romania and the Paris Peace Conference (1919): Actors, Scenarios, Circulation of Knowledge*, Special issue of the *Journal of Romanian Studies*, 1, no. 2 (2019): 9–152.
42 Norman Stone, *The Eastern Front, 1914–1917* (London: Penguin, 1998); Maria Bucur, "Between the Mother of the Wounded and the Virgin of Jiu: Romanian Women and the Gender of Heroism during the Great War," *Journal of Women's History*, 12, no. 2 (2000), 30–56; Glenn E. Torrey, *The Romanian Battlefront in World War I* (Lawrence: University Press of Kansas, 2011); Claudiu-Lucian Topor and Alexander Rubel (eds), *"The Unknown War" from Eastern Europe: Romania between Allies and Enemies (1916–1918)* (Iaşi: Editura Universităţii "Alexandru Ioan Cuza", 2016).

modest Romanian nation-state to a European level of prosperity and civilization and transform it into Greater Romania encompassing all Romanians."[43] Others have recognized the central role Nicolae Titulescu played in Balkan diplomacy, the League of Nations, and in building the pro-French alliances of the 1920s.[44]

The extent to which Romania had a choice about allying itself with Nazi Germany remains contested. Andreas Hillgruber's 1954 study argued that a German-Romanian alliance was "natural" given the German roots of the Hohenzollern dynasty and had only been derailed by the First World War and Titulescu's subsequent foreign policy. He emphasized trade relations—especially Romanian oil—as the driving force between Romania's alliance with Germany and almost completely ignored the ideological implications of the alliance.[45] In 1989 Dov Lungu's more balanced work stressed Romania's precarity as a small state caught up in the growing tensions in Europe, the unsatisfactory nature of the alliance with the Soviets, and how few choices the Romanians really had by 1940.[46] Eleven years later, Rebecca Haynes argued that pro-German sentiment ran much deeper in Romania than had previously been thought, and that Romanians *chose* Germany over France rather than being forced into the alliance.[47]

Fascists—in particular legionaries—were frequently accused during the interwar period of having been financed by Nazi Germany. The 1971 study by Mihai Fătu and Ion Spălățelu labeled the Legion a "terrorist movement" and argued that fascism had no popular basis in Romania but was an "instrument of German Nazism."[48] Most legionaries denied these accusations, and Armin Heinen found only a single German donation to Ștefan Tătărescu, the leader of Romania's National Socialist Party, in

---

43 Keith Hitchins, *Ionel Brătianu: Romania* (London: Haus Publishing, 2011), ix; Sherman David Spector, *Romania at the Paris Peace Conference: A Study of the Diplomacy of Ioan I.C. Brătianu* (Iași: Center for Romanian Studies, 1995). In a more nationalist vein, see also Vasile Pușcaș and Ionel N. Sava (eds), *Trianon, Trianon!: Un secol de mitologie politică revizionistă* (Cluj-Napoca: Editura Școala Ardeleană, 2020).
44 Cristian Popișteanu, *România și Antanta Balcanică* (București: Editura Politică, 1968); Dov B. Lungu, *Romania and the Great Powers, 1933–1940* (Durham: Duke University Press, 1989), 15–99; Keith Hitchins, *Rumania* (London: Clarendon Press, 1994), 426–37.
45 Andreas Hillgruber, *Hitler, König Carol und Marschall Antonescu: die deutsch-rumänischen Beziehungen, 1938–1944* (Wiesbaden: Franz Steiner Verlag, 1954).
46 Lungu, *Romania and the Great Powers*, 99–228.
47 Rebecca Haynes, *Romanian Policy Towards Germany, 1936–40* (Basingstoke: Palgrave Macmillan, 2000).
48 Mihai Fătu and Ion Spălățelu, *Garda de Fier: Organizație teroristă de tip fascist* (București: Editura Politică, 1980), 10.

1934.[49] Captured German archives held in Britain show that the Nazis in fact subsidized a range of far-right newspapers throughout the 1930s, from *Calendarul* to *Porunca vremii*, but still do not mention financing fascist parties directly.[50] Holly Case's *Between States* (2009) pushes the debate forward by emphasizing "the European idea as emerging from relations between neighboring states" rather than as a product of Great Power politics.[51] Posing the question in terms of Romanian agency masks the very real cleavages across Europe as a whole. Liberals in Romania developed policy in tandem with their counterparts in France and Germany, while the far right pursued a common agenda in all three countries. Recent studies on Romanians studying abroad have highlighted how the ideological polarization of Europe shaped Romanian realities through individual biographies.[52] Saxons also travelled to Nazi Germany during this period, and more research is needed into the international journeys and transnational ties of other minority groups.[53]

Influenced by world systems theory and dependency theory, Katherine Verdery's 1983 history of a Transylvanian village argued that the region became "underdeveloped" because of patterns of industrialization across the Habsburg Empire after 1800, the evolution of Transylvania as a supplier of raw material for industrializing Hungary after 1867, and the failure to attract foreign investment during the 1920s.[54] In contrast, Kenneth Jowitt and Daniel Chirot took the idea that Romania really was backward at face value and tried to show how such a situation had emerged.[55] Similarly, both Lucian Boia and Oliver Jens Schmitt have grounded their

---

49 Armin Heinen, *Legiunea "Arhanghelul Mihail": Mișcare socială și organizație politică* (București: Humanitas, 2006), 225.
50 The National Archives (UK), German Foreign Ministry Archives, Press Department, German Press in Romania, GFM 33/3464/9602, Serial 9601, E676783–E676835.
51 Case, *Between States*, 7.
52 Diana Georgescu, "Excursions into National Specificity and European Identity: Mihail Sebastian's Interwar Travel Reportage," in *Under Eastern Eyes: A Comparative Introduction to East European Travel Writing on Europe*, eds. Wendy Bracewell and Alex Drace-Francis (Budapest: Central European University Press, 2008), 293–324; Irina Nastasă-Matei, *Educație, politică și propaganda: Studenți români în Germania nazistă* (Cluj-Napoca: Editura Școala Ardeleană, 2016).
53 Georgescu, *The Eugenic Fortress*.
54 Katherine Verdery, *Transylvanian Villagers: Three Centuries of Political, Economic, and Ethnic Change* (Berkeley: University of California Press, 1983), 130–40, 195–210, 276–86.
55 Kenneth Jowitt, *Social Change in Romania, 1860–1940: A Debate on Development in a European Nation* (Berkeley: University of California, Institute of International Studies, 1978); Daniel Chirot (ed), *The Origins of Backwardness in Eastern Europe: Economics and Politics from the Middle Ages until the Early Twentieth Century* (Berkeley: University of California Press, 1989).

observations that "something isn't right in Romania" by unpacking historical trends that did not go quite as they should have.[56] Whereas both Boia and Schmitt focus on cultural history, Bogdan Murgescu's detailed analysis of economic statistics builds on Chirot's narrative in a different way. He argues that Romania lagged behind the rest of Europe economically not only because it suffered from the same macro-economic influences that plagued all European economies during these decades but also because of inopportune policies regarding protectionism and exports.[57] Murgescu's data resonates with discussions of Romanian political economy written under state socialism and more recently by historians in Germany.[58] The story remains that of a small state navigating international currents beyond its control but the questions have shifted from "what can Romania do for us?" and "was Romania a victim of Great Power politics?" to "how did Romanian realities fit into transnational puzzles?" One question that has rarely been asked is how Romanians came to think of themselves as backward. *Pace* Chirot and Boia, the notion of backwardness is itself neo-colonial and problematic, and we need more histories that explore backwardness as a construct, as several recent historians have done.[59]

The Collapse of Democracy

Turning from a transnational story to a national one, the most enduring narrative is that of the collapse of democracy.[60] Writing during 1941, the communist activist Lucrețiu Pătrășcanu argued that the parliamentary

---

56 Lucian Boia, *De ce este România altfel?* (București: Humanitas, 2012); Oliver Jens Schmitt, *România în 100 de ani: Bilanțul unui veac de istorie* (București: Humanitas, 2018).
57 Bogdan Murgescu, *România și Europa: Acumularea decalajelor economice (1500–2010)* (Iași: Polirom, 2010), 205–314.
58 Ioan Saizu, *Politica economică a României între 1922 și 1928* (București: Editura Academiei Republicii Socialiste România, 1981); Dietmar Müller, *Agrarpopulismus in Rumänien: Programmatik und Regierungspraxis der Bauernpartei und der Nationalbäuerlichen Partei Rumäniens in der Zwischenkriegszeit* (Sankt Augustin: Gardez! Verlag, 2001); Angela Harre, *Wege in die Moderne: Entwicklungsstrategien rumänischer Ökonomen im 19. und 20. Jahrhundert* (Wiesbaden: Harrassowitz Verlag, 2009).
59 Mitu, *National Identity of Romanians in Transylvania*; Alex Drace-Francis, *The Traditions of Invention: Romanian Ethnic and Social Stereotypes in Historical Context* (Leiden: Brill, 2013); Diana Mishkova and Roumen Daskalov, "'Forms without Substance': Debates on the Transfer of Western Models to the Balkans", in *Entangled Histories of the Balkans*, Vol. 2: Transfers of Political Ideologies and Institutions, eds. Roumen Daskalov and Diana Mishkova (Leiden: Brill, 2013), 1–98; Vintilă Mihăilescu, *De ce este România astfel: Avatarurile excepționalismului românesc* (Iași: Polirom, 2017).
60 Roland Clark, "Interwar Romania: Enshrining Ethnic Privilege", in *Interwar East Central Europe, 1918–1941*, ed. Sabrina Ramet (London: Routledge, 2020), 144–77.

system disappeared as soon as it had outlived its usefulness to wealthy capitalists. Pătrășcanu maintained that the bankers controlled Romanian industry until the Great Depression crippled the banking industry in 1931. Whereas capitalists had been well represented by Brătianu's National Liberal Party (PNL) during the 1920s, increasing state regulation and the state's role as the largest consumer of industrial goods meant that the great industrialists gradually turned to Carol II's camarilla as the best way to guarantee their economic success. By 1938 "the royal dictatorship," Pătrășcanu wrote, "was the political expression of the interests of the great landholders and the leaders of industry. It thus had a decidedly economic basis."[61] Carol's unpopular rule relied too heavily on bureaucrats and army officers, however, and with no popular support was easily pushed aside by the fascists who, Pătrășcanu claimed, had German support. Despite its economic determinism and occasional flights of fancy, Pătrășcanu's narrative contains a number of elements that have endured in subsequent histories—a corrupt PNL, the importance of finance capital and industrialization, a superstitious and disaffected peasantry alienated from the political process, fascism as the pawn of cynical elites, and the personal ambitions of King Carol II undermining the legitimacy of parliament.

The most popular explanation for the collapse of parliamentary democracy emphasizes the failure of successive governments to win the support of rural voters through land reform and effective agrarian policies. This frame was first expressed during the interwar period by David Mitrany and Virgil Madgearu, then developed further by Hugh Seton-Watson in *Eastern Europe Between the Wars* (1945).[62] It was one of Seton-Watson's students, Henry Roberts, who crafted the authoritative version of this framework, which shaped Romanian studies in the West for several decades. Roberts conducted his research in Romania during 1944 and 1945, submitting his conclusions as a PhD dissertation in 1948. "The weak popular support of most of the parties, together with the extravagance of interparty squabbles," Roberts said, "had the inevitable consequence of increasing political indifference among the mass of the people and of lending a certain plausibility to the claims of those who stood 'above politics'."[63] The result, he argued, was the rise of fascism and the royal dictatorship. Roberts proved

---

61   Lucrețiu Pătrășcanu, *Sous trois dictatures* (Paris: Ed. Jean Vitiano, 1946).
62   David Mitrany, *The Land and the Peasant in Rumania: The War and Agrarian Reform (1917–21)* (London: H. Milford, 1930); Virgil N. Madgearu, *Evoluția economiei românești: după războiul mondial* (București: Independența Economică, 1940); Seton-Watson, *Eastern Europe between the Wars*.
63   Henry L. Roberts, *Rumania: Political Problems of an Agrarian State* (New Haven: Yale University Press, 1951), 92.

his case through a detailed analysis of economic data and written documents from the period, bringing a new level of professionalism to English-language writing about Romania. Roberts was so successful that almost all of the synthetic histories of Eastern Europe written between 1956 and 1998 drew heavily on his and Hugh Seton-Watson's accounts, including Joseph Rothschild's influential *East Central Europe between the Two World Wars* (1974).[64]

In the context of the Cold War, Romanian émigré historians of fascism described a backward, peasant country riddled with antisemitism that turned to fascism because of ignorance and superstition. Eugen Weber wrote in 1965 that "whereas Western fascist movements were generally a-religious or antireligious, [Codreanu's] was a religious revival, or, perhaps more correctly, a revivalist movement with strong religious overtones." He compared the Legion to "novel revivalist churches" in Africa, which used religious innovations to establish a new social and political order.[65] One early historian even justified separating the Legion from the study of other fascist movements on the dubious grounds that in Romania the Legion developed "within the framework of a completely Orientalized way of life," and "as a result of Oriental despotism."[66] Nicholas Nagy-Talavera's account was likewise centered in isolated villages and recounted the author's childhood awe in the face of towering legionaries dressed as *haiduci* (bandits) with turkey feathers in their hats, riding white horses and prophesying a new spiritual age.[67] Béla Vago further reinforced the themes of backwardness and violence in his edited collection

---

64   Robert Lee Wolff, *The Balkans in Our Time* (Cambridge, MA: Harvard University Press, 1956); Joseph Rothschild, *East Central Europe between the Two World Wars* (Seattle: University of Washington Press, 1974); Peter F. Sugar, Donald Warren Treadgold, Charles Jelavich, and Barbara Jelavich, *A History of East Central Europe* (Seattle: University of Washington Press, 1977); Barbara Jelavich, *History of the Balkans: Twentieth Century*, vol. 2 (Cambridge: Cambridge University Press, 1983); Robin Okey, *Eastern Europe 1740–1985: Feudalism to Communism*, Second Edition (Minneapolis: University of Minnesota Press, 1986); Ivan T. Berend, *Decades of Crisis: Central and Eastern Europe before World War II* (Berkeley: University of California Press, 1998).

65   Eugen Weber, "Romania," in *The European Right: A Historical Profile*, eds. Hans Rogger and Eugen Weber (Berkeley: University of California Press, 1965), 523, 534. Zeev Barbu and Stephen Fischer-Galati both also followed this line of interpretation. Zeev Barbu, "Rumania," in *European Fascism*, ed. S. J. Woolf (London: Weidenfeld and Nicolson, 1968), 146–166; Stephen Fischer-Galati, "Fascism in Romania," in *Native Fascism in the Successor States 1918–1945*, ed. Peter F. Sugar (Santa Barbara: ABC-Clio, 1971), 113.

66   Emanuel Turczynski, "The Background of Romanian Fascism," in *Native Fascism*, ed. Peter Sugar, 102, 104.

67   Nicholas M. Nagy-Talavera, *The Green Shirts and the Others: A History of Fascism in Hungary and Rumania* (Stanford: Hoover Institution Press, 1970).

of British Foreign Office documents on interwar Romania, a book which once again focused on the rise of fascism.[68]

Stephen Fischer-Galați's *Twentieth-Century Rumania* (1970) added much needed nuance to the story by reminding us that Jews were not the only minorities in the country and legionaries not the only people involved in right-wing politics. Fischer-Galați raised the question of "whether a democratic regime representative of the interests of all inhabitants of Rumania could ever have been established in that country."[69] Drawing explicitly on Roberts, he concluded that the nationalist and corrupt political culture had made no attempt at reconciling elites and peasants, Romanians and minorities, center and peripheries into a functioning political organism. He insisted that nationalism and antisemitism were core ideologies of interwar Romania but noted that the king chose to support the extremist National Christian Party (PNC) when he was faced with a choice between Iuliu Maniu and Corneliu Zelea Codreanu after the 1937 elections, destabilizing democracy and making a royal dictatorship possible. His decision, Fischer-Galați wrote, was driven by the knowledge that both Maniu and Codreanu wanted him to abdicate or at least to limit his power significantly. In the end ideology was less important than Carol's personal ambitions and his bank accounts.[70]

Rejecting the assertion that there was anything unusual or peripheral about Romanian fascism, in 1986 Armin Heinen argued persuasively that the Legion was a fascist social movement comparable to German Nazism or Italian Fascism, with a mass following and clear political goals.[71] Heinen's approach to the Legion as a movement waned over the next two decades, as historians focused increasingly on the person of Codreanu himself. Encouraged by the blossoming literature on European antisemitism and the Holocaust, Radu Ioanid argued that antisemitism lay at the core of Romanian fascism. Antisemitism, he showed, was deeply rooted within Romanian culture but suddenly became a substantial political movement in the 1920s.[72] In 1993 Francisco Veiga used oral history interviews to portray

---

68 Béla Vago, *The Shadow of the Swastika: The Rise of Fascism and Anti-Semitism in the Danube Basin, 1936–1939* (Farnborough: Saxon House for the Institute of Jewish Affairs, 1975).
69 Stephen Fischer-Galați, *Twentieth Century Rumania* (New York: Columbia University Press, 1970), 41–2.
70 Ibid., 58–9. On the influence of Carol's finances, see Robert Arnold, *King Carol's Personal Fortune and its Influence on Romania's Economic Negotiations with Germany 1937–1940* (PhD dissertation, Oxford University, 2008).
71 Heinen, *Legiunea "Arhanghelul Mihail."*
72 Radu Ioanid, *The Sword of the Archangel: Fascist Ideology in Romania*, transl. Peter Heinegg (Irvington, NY: Columbia University Press, 1990).

Codreanu as a political actor with little formal power and showed how his message and tactics mutated to take full advantage of the weaknesses of his opponents and the changing grievances of his followers.[73] Constantin Iordachi then revived the emphasis on peasant superstition that dominated the 1960s but did so in a more sophisticated manner that has been echoed by both Sandu Tudor and Oliver Jens-Schmitt.[74] Iordachi argued that messianic ideas about national regeneration found in nineteenth-century Romanian nationalism gathered legionaries around Codreanu as a leader endowed with unique charismatic qualities.[75] The stories told by Ioanid and Iordachi ground fascism so deeply in Romanian culture that the collapse of democracy appears almost a foregone conclusion.

Heinen was the only historian of fascism who paid much attention to the mainstream political parties, but all of these accounts assumed that ultimately the success or failure of fascism lay in the ability of the Liberals and the Peasantists to resist authoritarianism. Keith Hitchins summarized this position beautifully in 1994, arguing that by the 1930s "the leading democratic parties seemed to have lost much of their *élan* of the preceding decade. They proved incapable of withstanding the assault from both within and outside the country and acquiesced in the establishment of Carol's dictatorship in 1938, an event which marked the end of the democratic experiment in Rumania."[76] Hitchins provided clear and useful narratives of intellectual debates, economics, politics, and foreign policy during the interwar period. As he argued, the challenges facing Romanian elites after 1918 were substantial, and he helpfully showed how themes that continue to characterize the historiography—Romania as a small state, industrialization, the agrarian problem, democracy vs. authoritarianism, and pro-French vs. pro-German foreign policy—were all debated passionately during the 1920s and 1930s.

Subsequent historians have been less enthusiastic about the democratic credentials of the major parties. Hans Christian Maner's 1997 study of the parliamentary system emphasized that the country's "democracy" had not been healthy from the start. He noted how the 1923 constitution

---

73   Francisco Veiga, *Istoria Gărzii de Fier 1919–1941: mistica ultranaționalismului*, transl. Marian Ștefănescu (București: Humanitas, 1993).
74   Traian Sandu, *Un fascisme roumain: Histoire de la Garde de fer* (Paris: Perrin, 2014); Oliver Jens Schmitt, *Corneliu Zelea Codreanu: ascensiunea și căderea "Căpitanului"* (București: Humanitas, 2017).
75   Constantin Iordachi, *Charisma, Politics and Violence: The Legion of the "Archangel Michael" in Inter-war Romania* (Trondheim: Trondheim Studies on East European Cultures and Societies, 2004); *Martyrdom to Purification: The Fascist Faith of the Legion 'Archangel Michael' in Romania, 1927–1941* (London: Routledge, 2020).
76   Hitchins, *Rumania*, 378.

and the electoral laws of 1926 concentrated power firmly in the hands of the government and argued that Gheorghe Tătărescu's cabinets between 1934 and 1937 so discredited parliamentary democracy that "an openly authoritarian regime was the only way out."[77] Governments of the 1930s were already ruling in such an authoritarian manner that Carol was simply continuing a process begun long before the royal dictatorship. Whereas Maner's argument focused heavily on the Tătărescu regime, in 2001 Dietmar Müller turned his attention to the National Peasantist governments between 1928 and 1933. Not only did they fail to deliver on their promises to rural voters, Müller argued, but like the Liberals their policies were impractical and poorly thought through.[78] The following year Antoine Roger explained that the National Peasantist reluctance to push through a major new program of reform stemmed from the abject failure of the Liberal attempt "to mold society as they wished" between 1922 and 1928.[79] The programs of both the Liberals and the Peasantists had failed by 1934, and Roger portrayed Tătărescu's regime as a time of exploring alternative, nationalist options, which by now both the Carlists and the legionaries were also promoting. All three scholars laid the blame for the collapse of democracy firmly with the dysfunctional nature of the parliamentary system.

Dylan Riley shifted the narrative away from Bucharest politicians in 2010, arguing that the rural associations, cultural circles, and credit institutions established in the nineteenth century created an "agrarian civil society" that mobilized behind fascism when the failure of the ruling parties to win popular support became manifest at the beginning of the 1930s. Riley maintains that the rise of fascism exposed the weakness of parliamentary politics, providing an opening for the king to introduce a more authoritarian style of government.[80] Riley's position has been supported by Sorin Radu and Oliver Jens Schmitt, who argue that after the Great Depression "an often overlooked parallel society emerged in the rural area, under the guidance of social and ideological forces which openly rejected the existing political order."[81] The volume of case studies edited by Radu and Schmitt confirms that peasants were indeed involved in

---

77 Hans-Christian Maner, *Parlamentarismus in Rumänien (1930–1940): Demokratie im autoritären Umfeld* (München: R. Oldenbourg Verlag, 1997), 510.
78 Müller, *Agrarpopulismus in Rumänien*.
79 Antoine Roger, *Fascistes, communistes et paysans: Sociologie des mobilisations identitaires roumaines, 1921–1989* (Bruxelles: Université de Bruxelles, 2002), 141.
80 Dylan J. Riley, *The Civic Foundations of Fascism in Europe: Italy, Spain, and Romania, 1870–1945* (Baltimore: Johns Hopkins University Press, 2010), 113–48.
81 Sorin Radu and Oliver Jens Schmitt, "Introduction," in *Politics and Peasants in Interwar Romania*, eds. Sorin Radu and Oliver Jens Schmitt, 21.

party politics, and mobilizing rural voters could mean the difference between winning and losing an election. At the same time, peasants had their own, often local agendas and voted accordingly.[82]

Throughout the 1930s right-wing authoritarianism enjoyed the support of a number of prominent intellectuals, such as Mircea Eliade, Emil Cioran, Constantin Noica, and others. Norman Manea raised the question of Eliade's fascist past in 1990, and Zigu Ornea laid out the full extent of the problem in 1995.[83] Since then historians interested in the collapse of democracy narrative have repeatedly asked themselves how so many great minds could have supported such an evil ideology. Regardless of whether it celebrates them or condemns them as fascists, one inherent problem in this genre is that it presupposes that these men—and they were overwhelmingly men—were genuinely geniuses. A much more interesting question would be why they came to be seen and celebrated as geniuses to the exclusion of others, as Katherine Verdery did in *National Ideology Under Socialism* (1991).[84] The answer to their political choices, it seems, lay in the structure of intellectual life in interwar Romania. One study after another reflects the same central themes: a rapidly expanding system of higher education that nonetheless failed to provide jobs for talented intellectuals, the influence of a handful of charismatic right-wing mentors, the ascendency of fascism in Europe, nationalist presuppositions that became more and more important to articulate, the appeal of modernism, and a fashion for "spirituality" all attracted young Romanian intellectuals to the far right. At the same time, each study reveals a host of individual factors that are far from generalizable. Each person arrived at fascism along a different path and with varying degrees of commitment.[85] Moreover, as Ionuț Butoi shows in his recent microhistory of

---

82 Radu, Schmitt (eds), *Politics and Peasants*. See also Cornel Micu, *From Peasants to Farmers? Agrarian Reforms and Modernisation in Twentieth-Century Romania: A Case Study: Bordei Verde Commune in Brăila County* (Frankfurt am Main: Peter Lang, 2012).

83 Norman Manea, *On Clowns: The Dictator and the Artist* (London: Faber and Faber, 1994), 91–124; Zigu Ornea, *Anii treizeci: Extrema dreaptă românească* (București: Editura Fundației Culturale Române, 1995).

84 Verdery, *National Ideology Under Socialism*, 256–318.

85 Alexandre Laignel-Lavastine, *Cioran, Eliade, Ionesco: l'oubli du fascisme : trois intellectuels roumains dans la tourmente du siècle* (Paris: PUF, 2002); Florin Țurcanu, *Mircea Eliade: le prisonnier de l'histoire* (Paris: Découverte, 2003); Alexandru D. Popescu, *Petre Țuțea: Between Sacrifice and Suicide* (Aldershot: Ashgate, 2004); Marta Petreu, *An Infamous Past: E. M. Cioran and the Rise of Fascism in Romania*, transl. Bogdan Aldea (Chicago: Ivan R. Dee, 2005); Philip Vanhaelemeersch, *A Generation "without Beliefs" and the Idea of Experience in Romania (1927–1934)* (Boulder: East European Monographs, 2006); Ilinca Zarifopol-Johnston, (ed) *Sear-*

Mircea Vulcănescu, fascism was not the only option, and Orthodox Christian youth groups or Dimitrie Gusti's sociological teams were equally likely destinations for young nationalist intellectuals.[86] The study of right-wing intellectuals mirrors the evolution of the collapse of democracy narrative more generally. Few of the main contours of the story have changed significantly since 1948, but the importance of detail and nuance is becoming ever clearer as what used to be a straight-forward story reveals itself to have been remarkably complex.

The March of Progress

Relatively few historians writing under state socialism specialized in the interwar period, most focusing primarily on medieval and early modern history.[87] Gheorghe Platon's textbook *The History of Modern Romania* (1985) ends with the First World War, reflecting the reluctance of the regime to discuss the recent past.[88] It was the vice-president of the Romanian Academy, Mihail Roller, who first introduced a communist framework for the interwar period through strategic appointments to key academic posts, by publishing large collections of primary sources, and through his 1947 *History of Romania*. Roller and his collaborators emphasized class struggle as the engine of history, the positive benefits Russia and the Soviet Union had brought to Romania, and the harmful impact of the West and of bourgeois liberalism in general. They also highlighted the

---

ching for Cioran (Bloomington: Indiana University Press, 2009); Marta Petreu, *Diavolul și ucenicul său : Nae Ionescu—Mihail Sebastian* (Iași: Editura Polirom, 2009); Idem, *De la Junimea la Noica: studii de cultură românească* (Iași: Polirom, 2011); Boia, *Capcanele istoriei;* Antonio Momoc, *Capcanele politice ale sociologiei interbelice: Școala gustiană între carlism și legionarism* (București: Curtea Veche, 2012); Bejan, *Intellectuals and Fascism*.

86 Butoi, *Mircea Vulcănescu*.
87 Lajos Jordáky and Keith Hitchins, "The History of the Habsburg Monarchy (1789–1918) in Romanian Historiography since 1945," *Austrian History Yearbook*, 4 (1968): 303–34; Paul Michelson, "Themes in Modern and Contemporary Romanian Historiography," in S. J. Kirschbaum (ed), *East European History* (Columbus: Slavica Publishers, 1988), 27–40; Frederick Kellogg, *A History of Romanian Historical Writing* (Bakersfield: Charles Schlacks Jr, 1990), 52–70; Pompiliu Teodor, *Introducere în istoria istoriografiei din România* (Cluj-Napoca: Editura Accent, 2002), 112–127. For a comprehensive bibliography of Romanian histories of the interwar period written between 1944 and 1969 see Robert Deutsch, *Istoricii și știința istorică din România, 1944–1969* (București: Editura Științifică, 1970), 267–344.
88 Gheorghe Platon, *Istoria modernă a României* (București: Editura Didactică și Pedagogică, 1985).

struggles of the Romanian Communist Party (PCR) while minimizing the role of the Church and demonizing the monarchy.[89]

In 1951, Gheorghe Gheorghiu-Dej argued that interwar Romania had been "a colony of Anglo-Franco-American imperialism," with the bourgeoisie and the great landholders working together to keep the working classes under control. Gheorghiu-Dej identified the Bolshevik revolution in Russia as the motivation for the wave of strikes in the early 1920 but saw the rest of the decade as a time when the bourgeoisie and the landholders went on the "counter-offensive" alongside "reformist traitors" to take the wind out of the revolutionary movement, eventually financing fascism as a way to crush the workers.[90] By 1959, following Roller's fall from grace, de-Stalinization and a purge of the PCR, Gheorghiu-Dej's narrative had shifted to one of progress.[91] He now characterized the interwar as a period of "opportunism and reformism," but also one of a growing awareness among workers that communism was the country's only solution. Gheorghiu-Dej emphasized the Bolshevik revolution in Russia, the Fifth Party Congress in Moscow at which the PCR aligned itself with Stalin's geopolitical aims, and the strikes of 1920 and 1933 as moments of "awakening" for Romanian workers and of progress towards the victory of the PCR.[92] Earlier labor organizing among Romanians had been ineffective because it lacked the "revolutionary" focus of the PCR.[93]

Historians worked hard to confirm his story over the next few years, with an emphasis on the role of the PCR over and above that of peasant

---

89 Mihail Roller (ed), *Istoria României* (București: Editura de Stat, 1947); Boia, *History and Myth*, 70-3; Liviu Pleșa, "Mihail Roller și 'Stalinizarea' istoriografiei românești," *Annales Univeristatis Apulensis, Series Historica*, 10, no. 1 (2006): 165–77; Francesco Zavatti, *Writing History in a Propaganda Institute: Political Power and Network Dynamics in Communist Romania* (Stockholm: Södertörn University, 2016), 115-56.
90 Gh. Gheorghiu-Dej, *30 de ani de luptă a partidului sub steagul lui Lenin și Stalin* (București: Editura Partidului Muncitoresc Român, 1951).
91 Vladimir Tismăneanu, *Stalinism for All Seasons: A Political History of Romanian Communism* (Berkeley: University of California Press, 2003), 148-86; Zavatti, *Writing History*, 163-90.
92 Gheorghe Gheorghiu-Dej, quoted in E. Drob, G. Florea, and I. Tudosescu, "Formarea și dezvoltarea conștiinței politice socialiste a clasei muncitoare din țara noastră," in Institutul de Filozofie al Academiei RPR (ed), *Dezvoltarea conștiinței socialiste în Republica Populară Română* (București: Editura Academiei Republicii Populare Române, 1961), 96-9.
93 L. Fodor and L. Vaida, *Contribuții la istoria mișcării sindicale din Transilvania (1848-1917)* (Cluj: Editura Consiliului Central al Sindicatelor, 1957), 115-6.

movements or foreign assistance.⁹⁴ In contrast with the workers, they insisted, interwar peasants were unenlightened. They were "always tricked by 'politics,' deceived by newspapers, swindled at the markets by capitalist merchants, exploited and oppressed."⁹⁵ Despite horrific suffering, it was apparently only communist activists who convinced peasants to "ally themselves with the workers" and to engage in occasional revolts against capitalist oppression.⁹⁶ Writing in 1955, Dionisie Ionescu described an independent peasant revolt in Bacău county during 1936/37, but his colleagues emphasized that peasants were repeatedly defrauded of their land in progressive stages during the 1920s and 1930s.⁹⁷ The importance of the Romanian Communist Party to framing the interwar story became evident in 1963 when the History Institute of the Soviet Union Academy of Sciences attempted to write a history of modern Romania, only for it to be bitterly rejected by the Romanian Academy for emphasizing the importance of Russian influence at the expense of organic, local communist organizing.⁹⁸

The assertion of Romanian independence from the Soviet Union from 1964 onwards consolidated the centrality of national ideology for historical narratives, a move seen most clearly in the new emphasis on

---

94 Klaus P. Beer, "Die Interdependenz von Geschichtswissenschaft und Politik in Rumänien von 1945 bis 1980. Die Historiographie über den Zeitraum von 1918 bis 1945," *Jahrbücher für Geschichte Osteuropas*, 32, no. 2 (1984): 243–48. Examples include Institutul de Istorie a Partidului de pe lângă CC al PMR, *Greva generală din România, 1920* (București: Editura Politică, 1960); *Din lupta PCR pentru închegarea alianței clasei muncitoare cu țărănimea muncitoare în bătălia pentru reforma agrară din 1944–1945*, vol. 1 (București: Editura de Stat pentru Literatură Politică, 1961); Titu Georgescu, *De la greva generală la crearea PCR: Lupta pentru clarificarea politică, ideologică și organizatorică din mișcarea muncitorească în preajma creării PCR: octombrie 1920–mai 1921* (București: Editura Științifica, 1962); Titu Georgescu and Mircea Ioanid (eds), *Presa PCR și organizațiilor sale de masa, 1921–1944: Prezentare bibliografică* (București: Editura Științifică, 1963); Ion Popescu-Puțuri and Nicolae Goldberger (eds), *1933: Luptele revoluționare ale muncitorilor ceferiști și petroliști* (București: Editura Politică, 1971).
95 Mihail Cernea, "Cu privire la procesul formării și dezvoltării conștiinței politice socialiste a țărănimii," in Institutul de Filozofie al Academiei RPR ed., *Dezvoltarea conștiinței socialiste în Republica Populară Română* (București: Editura Academiei Republicii Populare Române, 1961), 313.
96 Titu Georgescu and Ladislau Fodor, *Răscoala țăranilor din Valea Ghimeșului (1934)* (București: Editura Politică, 1960).
97 Dionisie Ionescu, "Ocuparea pământurilor moșierești în regiunea Bacău (fostele județe Bacău și Neamț)," in Institutul de Istorie a Partidului de pe Lângă CC al PMR ed., *Din lupta PCR pentru închegarea alianței clasei muncitoare cu țărănimea muncitoare în bătălia pentru reforma agrară din 1944–1945*, vol. 1 (București: Editura de Stat pentru Literatură Politică, 1961), 59–60. Compare Ionescu's account with the other essays in this volume, which never mention peasant resistance prior to 1944.
98 Zavatti, *Writing History*, 179–80.

the historically "Romanian" character of Bessarabia despite the fact that it was now its own Soviet Republic.[99] The idea that class struggle facilitated a steady movement of national progress framed most communist histories written under Ceaușescu. Mircea Mușat and Ion Ardeleanu's two-volume history of *Romania after the Great Union* (1968), for example, argued that,

> Romania continued to be a unitary national state and Romanians constituted an overwhelming majority of the country's population after those provinces found under foreign occupation were united with their ancestral home. ... The consolidation of the country's human and economic potential created the conditions necessary for the productive exploitation of the riches of the soil and minerals at a national level, accentuating the role of industry within the national economy.[100]

The primary benefactors of Greater Romania were the bourgeoisie, Mușat and Ardeleanu argued, but agrarian reforms, the building of railroads, and the growth and science and education laid the foundations for national prosperity, and industrialization created a new working class which made state socialism possible. Even the rise of fascism seems not to have phased Mușat and Ardeleanu, who suggested that the extreme right had no popular support and was simply a creation of the bourgeoisie. In support of this narrative, state publishing houses reprinted the writings of prominent left-wing figures from the interwar period, even recasting beloved nationalist intellectuals such as Nicolae Iorga as anti-fascists.[101] In 1975 Dumitru Șandru challenged the narrative of ever-greater suffering, replacing it with a whiggish story of gradual progress. Blending a detailed analysis of economic statistics with an account of communist activism, he argued that although they were insufficient, the land reforms of 1921–23 did improve the lives of the majority of peasants over the next twenty years.[102]

Not only is the communist story of progress empirically wrong in terms of economic growth, it raises ethical questions about whether the

---

99   Beer, "Die Interdependenz," 248–61; Zavatti, *Writing History*, 294–6.
100 Mircea Mușat and Ion Ardeleanu, *România după Marea Unire* vol. 2, Partea 1 (1918–1933) (București: Editura Științifică și Enciclopedică, 1986), v.
101 Boia, *History and Myth*, 75–6. For example, Titu Georgescu, *Nicolae Iorga împotriva hitlerismului* (București: Editura Științifică, 1966); *Intelectuali antifasciști în publicistica românească* (București: Editura Științifică, 1967); N. D. Cocea, *Jurnal* (București: Editura Politică, 1970); Ion Constantinescu, *Din însemnările unui fost reporter parlamentar: Camera deputaților, 1919–1939* (Bucharest: Editura Politică, 1973); C. G. Costa-Foru, *Din viața și opera unui mare democrat român* (Cluj-Napoca: Dacia, 1986);
102 Dumitru Șandru, *Reforma agrară din 1921 în România* (București: Editura Academiei Republicii Socialiste România, 1975). Șandru's narrative of progress was affirmed in Vasile Pușcaș and Vasile Vesa (eds), *Dezvoltare și modernizare în România interbelică 1919–1939* (București: Editura politică, 1988).

sufferings of one generation can be said to have been "worthwhile," because they paved the way to future prosperity. Historians who came of age under state socialism continued to promote this narrative after the regime collapsed, but it had effectively lost its appeal in its communist form by the beginning of the twenty-first century.[103]

Nation-Building and Centralization

While the narrative of progress was being promoted inside Romania, historians in the United States and Germany were developing a more complicated version of the collapse of democracy narrative around questions of regionalism, centralization, and the treatment of minorities. Irina Livezeanu's *Cultural Politics in Greater Romania* (1995)—originally written as her PhD dissertation in 1986—argued that bureaucrats, politicians, teachers, and journalists exploited "ethnic nationalist ideology" to facilitate the incorporation of the new territories of Transylvania, Crișana, Maramureș, Bukovina, Bessarabia, the Banat, and Dobruja into Greater Romania after 1918. They promoted Romanian culture in schools and universities to the exclusion of minority languages and literatures and sent teachers and administrators from the Old Kingdom into the provinces to replace existing staff. Coupled with overcrowding and administrative problems in the universities, the state's nation-building project produced a generation of ultranationalist students who used violence and intimidation to establish fascism.[104] Subsequent research has confirmed Livezeanu's conclusions about problems in the universities. Dragoș Sdrobiș in particular argues that the student violence of the early 1920s was symptomatic of wider social problems, including xenophobic nationalism, fears of cultural inferiority, anger at political corruption, an underfunded education system, and a surplus of unemployed intellectuals.[105]

Although she also drew on political speeches and journalistic manifestos which demonstrate beyond doubt how omnipresent the centralization narrative was, Livezeanu's narrative was based heavily on archival documents. Her sources reflected a bureaucrat's way of looking at the

---

103 For example, Nicolae N. Constantinescu, *Romania's Economic History: From the Beginnings to World War II* (București: Editura Academiei Române, 1994); Ion Bulei, *Scurtă istorie a Românilor* (București: Meronia, 1996).
104 Irina Livezeanu, *Cultural Politics in Greater Romania: Regionalism, Nation Building, and Ethnic Struggle, 1918–1930* (Ithaca: Cornell University Press, 1995).
105 Dragoș Sdrobiș, *Limitele meritocrației într-o societate agrară: Șomaj intelectual și radicalizare politică a tineretului în România interbelică* (Iași: Polirom, 2015). See also Roland Clark, *Holy Legionary Youth: Fascist Activism in Interwar Romania* (Ithaca: Cornell University Press, 2015).

world and the state's perspective on social problems. They thus marginalized the myriad of other stories that took place outside of the state's field of interest, and implied that historical actors were motivated primarily by a nation-building ideology when in fact this was just the language that individuals learned to use when interacting with the state in order to promote their own ambitions and personal rivalries. The narrative of nation-building and centralization has nonetheless been incredibly productive and has inspired a solid corpus of new and innovative research.

In 2001, Mariana Hausleitner documented the destruction of multicultural Bukovina during the 1920s, as the Romanian state systematically restricted expressions of Ukrainian, Jewish, German, and Polish culture in a process that culminated in the deportations and massacres of the Holocaust.[106] Alberto Basciani's analysis of the Romanianization of Bessarabia argues that not only was the state inconsistent in how it applied nation-building policies there, but that the process was complicated by geography and fears about communism.[107] Florian Kührer-Wielach's 2014 study of a parallel process in Transylvania reveals a quite different process at work there. With stronger democratic traditions and decades of experience resisting Magyarization by the Austro-Hungarians, ethnic Romanians in Transylvania worked to sabotage Bucharest's attempts at centralization, attempting to impose their own vision of what the relationship between regions and the nation-state should be. Ultimately neither side was completely victorious, the result being a complex compromise.[108]

Both Hausleitner and Kührer-Wielach note that "modernization"—and industrialization in particular—were core elements of national integration, but Kührer-Wielach argues that the Romanian Orthodox, Greek Catholic, and Roman Catholic Churches also played key roles in creating regional and national identities.[109] His argument builds on Hans-Christian Maner's pioneering study on ecclesiastical politics in 2007. Maner shows how confessional conflicts exacerbated attempts at nation-building, and representatives from different provinces inside each church also resisted Bucharest's centralizing tendencies. The Metropolitan of Transylvania,

---

106 Mariana Hausleitner, *Die Rumänisierung der Bukowina: die Durchsetzung des nationalstaatlichen Anspruchs Grossrumäniens 1918–1944* (München: Oldenbourg, 2001).
107 Alberto Basciani, *La difficile unione: la Bessarabia e la Grande Romania, 1918–1940* (Roma: Aracne, 2005).
108 Florian Kührer-Wielach, *Siebenbürgen ohne Siebenbürger?: Zentralstaatliche Integration und politischer Regionalismus nach dem Ersten Weltkrieg* (Munchen: De Gruyter Oldenbourg, 2014).
109 Ibid., 360.

Nicolae Bălan, for example, "maintained that the Orthodox Church is neither above the state, nor ruled by it. Based on Transylvanian tradition, he strongly insisted on the maintenance of ecclesiastical autonomy and decentralized decision-making."[110] At the same time that he defended the rights of Orthodoxy against Greek- and Roman Catholics, Bălan also encouraged both church and state to persecute minorities, including Jews, Freemasons, Baptists, Brethren, and Pentecostals. A host of histories documenting this persecution have appeared in recent years, telling the story from the victim perspective and portraying interwar Romania as a hostile, persecuting society.[111] The state deported some Protestants to Transnistria during the Holocaust, and as Ion Popa argues in *The Romanian Orthodox Church and the Holocaust* (2017), leading figures within the Orthodox Church promoted violent antisemitism and actively encouraged the state's genocidal project against the Jews.[112]

The Holocaust looms large in many of the narratives about centralization and nation-building. Vladimir Solonari in particular argues that the Holocaust in Transnistria was part of a larger project to transform Bessarabia into a "model province." Using deportations and mass murder, Romanian administrators hoped to "purify" the eastern provinces of undesired ethnic groups, just as they did through the population exchanges with Bulgaria.[113] Not only state officials were involved in the Holocaust. Comparing Romanian Bessarabia with Soviet Transnistria on the left bank of the Dniester River, Diana Dumitru claims that Bessarabians were so convinced by the state's antisemitic propaganda that the twenty years

---

110 Hans-Christian Maner, *Multikonfessionalität und neue Staatlichkeit: Orthodoxe, griechisch-katholische und römisch-katholische Kirche in Siebenbürgen und Altrumänien zwischen den Weltkriegen* (1918–1940) (Stuttgart: Franz Steiner Verlag, 2007), 346.

111 The most authoritative is Dorin Dobrincu and Danuț Mănăstireanu eds., *Omul evanghelic: O explorare a comunităților protestante românești* (Iași: Polirom, 2018). For an overview of the literature in English, see Paul Michelson, "The History of Romanian Evangelicals, 1918–1989: A Bibliographical Excursus," *Archiva Moldaviae*, 9 (2017): 191–234. For an attempt at a more balanced approach to Romanian church history, see Roland Clark, *Sectarianism and Renewal in 1920s Romania: The Limits of Orthodoxy and Nation-Building* (London: Bloomsbury, 2021).

112 Viorel Achim (ed), *Politica regimului Antonescu față de cultele neoprotestante: Documente* (Iași: Polirom, 2013); Ion Popa, *The Romanian Orthodox Church and the Holocaust* (Bloomington: Indiana University Press, 2017).

113 Vladimir Solonari, *Purifying the Nation: Population Exchange and Ethnic Cleansing in Nazi-Allied Romania* (Washington D.C.: Woodrow Wilson Center Press, 2009).

of Romanian rule transformed them into willing perpetrators of the Holocaust. Transnistrians, on the other hand, were more likely to help Jews during the Holocaust.[114]

Nationalism, antisemitism, and eugenics were core ideologies of the centralizing nation-state. Constantin Iordachi's recent book shows that nationalism and liberalism were intimately connected in Romanian politics from 1750 onwards, and that during the nineteenth century exclusion shadowed almost all discussions of extending civil rights.[115] Antisemitism bedeviled important intellectual debates in the interwar period and was the motivating force behind both political policies and parties.[116] Not just an influential set of ideas, antisemitism structured everyday practices that marginalized and discriminated against Jews.[117]

Historians of the Holocaust from Radu Ioanid to Jean Ancel have repeatedly emphasized the connection between organized antisemitism and the mass murders that began in 1940. At the same time, however, they also acknowledge that the Holocaust was only made possible by the unique combination of events between 1940 and 1943 that gave Romanian perpetrators the opportunities and means to carry out the killings.[118]

---

114 Diana Dumitru, *The State, Antisemitism, and Collaboration in the Holocaust: The Borderlands of Romania and the Soviet Union* (New York: Cambridge University Press, 2016).
115 Constantin Iordachi, *Liberalism, Constitutional Nationalism, and Minorities: The Making of Romanian Citizenship, c. 1750–1918* (Leiden: Brill, 2019).
116 Léon Volovici, *Nationalist Ideology and Anti-Semitism: The Case of Romanian Intellectuals in the 1930s* (Oxford: Pergamon Press, 1991); Carol Iancu, *Evreii din România: 1919–1938: De la emancipare la marginalizare* (București: Hasefer, 2000); Gabriel Asandului, *Istoria Evreilor din România (1866–1938)* (Iași: Institutul European, 2003); Andrei Oișteanu, *Inventing the Jew: Antisemitic Stereotypes in Romanian and Other Central East-European Cultures*, transl. Mirela Adăscăliței (Lincoln: University of Nebraska Press, 2009); Peter Manu and Horia Bozdoghină, *Polemica Paulescu: Știință, politică, memorie* (Bucharest: Curtea Veche, 2010); Horia Bozdoghină, *Antisemitismul lui A. C. Cuza în politica românească* (București: Curtea Veche, 2012); Irina Marin, *Peasant Violence and Antisemitism in Early Twentieth-Century Eastern Europe* (Basingstoke: Palgrave Macmillan, 2018).
117 Anca Filipovici and Attila Gidó (eds), *Trecutul prezent: Evreii din România: istorie, memorie, reprezentare* (Cluj-Napoca: Editura Institutului pentru Studierea Problemelor Minorităților Naționale, 2018).
118 Radu Ioanid, *The Holocaust in Romania: The Destruction of Jews and Gypsies Under the Antonescu Regime, 1940–1944* (Chicago: Ivan R. Dee, 2000), 5–61; Elie Wiesel et al., *Final Report of the International Commission on the Holocaust in Romania* (București: International Commission on the Holocaust in Romania, 2004), 19–56; Dennis Deletant, *Hitler's Forgotten Ally: Ion Antonescu and His Regime, Romania 1940–44* (New York: Palgrave Macmillan, 2006); Armin Heinen, *Rumänien, der Holocaust und die Logik der Gewalt* (München: R. Oldenbourg Verlag, 2007), 49–53; Jean Ancel, *The History of the Holocaust in Romania* (Lincoln: University of Nebraska Press, 2011), 25–70.

Alongside antisemitism were scientists and policy makers committed to creating an ethnically and socially "healthy" nation-state even if this involved sterilization and other restrictive measures aimed at eradicating "undesirable" traits in the population.[119] As Tudor Georgescu demonstrates, Romanian officials and doctors were not the only ones interested in eugenics, and the ideology shaped the development of Transylvanian Saxon communities throughout the 1930s.[120] Historians have been more hesitant to draw a straight line from eugenics to the Holocaust, but alongside historians of centralization and nation-building, they nonetheless emphasize that the same motivations and ideologies inspired both movements.

Beyond the Grand Narrative

A large number of new and hitherto inaccessible sources became available after the fall of the Ceaușescu dictatorship in December 1989. Western scholars now travel easily within Romania. Books, memoirs, diaries, and essay collections written by interwar intellectuals and politicians are republished and became easily accessible in most major research libraries in the country as well as in Western Europe and the United States. Historians, sociologists, and anthropologists began carrying out large-scale oral history projects on interwar Romanian history during the late 1990s and early 2000s. First the National Archives, then the archives of the Securitate, became accessible to historians. Yet despite the sudden increase in source material, the dominant frameworks of interwar history hardly changed. Their enduring success testifies to the quality of the works by pioneering historians such as Seton-Watson, Roller, Roberts, Hillgruber, Heinen, Hitchins, and Livezeanu. With the exception of Roller's nationalist account of the march of progress, the details established by these historians have survived just as well as the core elements of their general frameworks. At the same time, however, one wonders whether the failure of subsequent generations of historians to establish new frameworks points to a lack of imagination across the field as a whole. The cultural turn, the literary turn, the rise of gender history, the history of sexualities, histories of the body, ethnomusicology, the spatial turn, global history, environmental history, the history of animals, and other innovative new approaches that have transformed the writing of history over the past thirty

---

119 Maria Bucur, *Eugenics and Modernization* (Pittsburgh: University of Pittsburgh Press, 2002); Marius Turda (ed), *The History of East-Central European Eugenics, 1900–1945: Sources and Commentaries* (London: Bloomsbury Academic, 2015).
120 Georgescu, *The Eugenic Fortress*.

years have made remarkably little impact on the historiography of interwar Romania. The need for historians to read outside of their own fields and to adopt interdisciplinary methodologies is as urgent now as ever. Adapting ideas from studies of other times and places will allow us to see interwar Romania with new eyes and to discern new narratives running through the past.

Reading the past with an eye to the concerns of the twenty-first century also has the potential to generate new narratives. All of the earlier frameworks that continue to shape Romanian studies emerged out of the concerns of their eras. Seton-Watson and Roberts wrote with British interests in mind, Roller and Gheorghiu-Dej with a concern for spreading communist ideology, and Livezeanu with an awareness of the new approaches to nationalism and antisemitism that became popular during the 1980s. Verdery was influenced by world systems theory, a left-wing response to the inequalities created by global capitalism, and Heinen by social movement studies that emerged out of the new social movements of the 1960s. What might historians uncover today by interrogating gender binaries, asking about populism and radical right extremism, ethnic privilege, European integration, the interaction between humans and their environment, or the impact on new technologies of communication on the public sphere? All of these remain under-researched fields with great potential for future discoveries. Done well, asking today's questions of the past does not mean imposing our concerns onto the past but allowing the past to speak into the present in new ways.

Historians of interwar Romania have consistently struggled to portray plurality and to include ethnic and religious minorities within their narratives, Maria Bucur's *Heroes and Victims* (2010) being one of the few exceptions. Not only does Bucur manage to tell the story of Romanian, Hungarian, German, and Jewish memorialization, she also alerts us to a striking disconnect between state-sponsored narratives about the war and individual, family, or ethnic memories. Communities mourned their loved ones who perished in the First World War in different ways, and men and women played different roles in commemorations. Bucur's achievement is to unite the plurality of different voices into a single polyphonic narrative, as well as situating the interwar period within a longer temporal trajectory, from the 1880s to the 1990s.[121]

Other historians have shown parallel processes at work within Hungarian and Romanian communities, telling transnational stories that took

---

121 Maria Bucur, *Heroes and Victims: Remembering War in Twentieth-Century Romania* (Bloomington IN: Indiana University Press, 2010), 49–143.

place simultaneously in both nation-states.[122] In *Hungarian Religion, Romanian Blood* (2019), R. Chris Davis shows how sociological, religious, and nationalist discourses from three different communities—Romanian, Hungarian, and Csango—converged during the 1930s to threaten the very existence of the Csango people. Similarly, James Kapaló's history of Inochentism analyses how stories about a religious minority spread from newspapers into police reports and popular culture, resulting in the harsh repression of believers by the state. By refusing to rely on only one type of source Kapaló manages to analyze interactions between social groups and to expose how one body of sources influenced another. In doing so he lets us see interwar Romania through the eyes of a persecuted minority rather than only through the eyes of the state.[123]

Disempowered minorities are not the only people ignored by the dominant frameworks of interwar Romanian history. Whereas most historians have focused on the perspective of the Romanian state and the debates of economists, Máté Rigó has been able to shed new light on interwar history by following the fortunes of "Europe's top one percent." Contrary to what the dominant frameworks suggest, Rigó shows that Jewish industrialists actually did better in antisemitic Transylvania than in supposedly tolerant France, and that French hegemony in Eastern Europe was as much about economics as about geopolitics.[124]

Bucur, Davis, Kapaló, Rigó and others like them show that alternative frameworks are possible. Integrating the stories of women and of ethnic and religious minorities into those about Romanian men produces much richer, more sophisticated, and more accurate history, as does viewing the past from hitherto unexplored perspectives, such as those of Inochentists or industrialists. What could we learn about interwar Romania if we approached it from the perspective of non-human actors, such as wolves or forests, or if we took Jewish hymnals, carts or railway stations as our primary texts? How did the lives of people with physical or mental disabilities change during this period, and how was life as a pensioner different in 1940 compared to 1920? Did men who had sex with

---

122 Anders E. B. Blomqvist, Constantin Iordachi and Balázs Trencsényi (eds), *Hungary and Romania Beyond National Narratives: Comparisons and Entanglements* (Oxford: Peter Lang, 2013).
123 James A. Kapaló, *Inochentism and Orthodox Christianity: Religious Dissent in the Russian and Romanian Borderlands* (New York: Routledge, 2019). See also James Kapaló and Tatiana Vagramenko (eds), *Hidden Galleries: Material Religion in the Secret Police Archives in Central and Eastern Europe* (Münster: Lit Verlag, 2020).
124 Máté Rigó, *Imperial Elites after the Fall of Empires: Business Elites and States in Europe's East and West, 1867–1928* (PhD dissertation, Cornell University, 2016).

other men find their lifestyles constrained by the rise of right-wing nationalism in the late 1930s, or did the relative invisibility of homosexuality mean that things got neither better nor worse for them? To what extent did shifting geopolitical alliances, ethnic tensions, or changing technology impact the history of dance, and how did the rise of the oil industry change the lives of working-class youths? Which innovative new frameworks will find traction in the coming years is anyone's guess, but the vibrancy of alternative frameworks in the histories of other national contexts suggests that there is much still to be uncovered about interwar Romania that has hitherto been ignored or marginalized by the dominant frameworks in the field.

The Romanian Orthodox Church and its Financial Dealings in Post-Communism

Lavinia Stan and Lucian Turcescu

Abstract: *This article introduces the main sources of revenue and wealth of the dominant Romanian Orthodox Church as subventions from the state, the restitution of assets confiscated by the communist authorities, donations collected from various groups and individuals, money obtained for services and religious artifacts offered to believers, and other revenue-generating activities. It then discusses two instances in which the Orthodox Church has come under attack for the way it collects and uses money, the contributions it receives from the reserve fund of the government and the church's efforts to finance the building in downtown Bucharest of a monumental national cathedral. Finally, the article tests the degree of secularization in Romania, based on the observations of José Casanova and Vyacheslav Karpov, to measure if and how much the country has secularized, especially in light of the economic and financial aspects of church activity presented here.*

Secularization theorists have long argued that decreased religiosity and separation of state from religious institutions are a byproduct of increased modernization, urbanization, rationalization, and democratization.[1] Romania was considered by some to be no exception to this rule. Nevertheless, the collapse of the communist regime has brought high levels of religiosity and a questionable separation of church from state in the country. In this article, we adopt a new perspective on secularization by focusing our attention on the financial dealings of the majority Orthodox Church during communist times. In doing so, we will look to see how much this majority church has separated from the state, and thus provide some reflections on the country's degree of secularization in the process of democratization and modernization it has engaged in following the collapse of its communist regime in 1989.

---

1 Peter L. Berger, *The Sacred Canopy* (Garden City, NY: Doubleday, 1967); Steve Bruce (ed), *Religion and Modernization* (Oxford: Oxford University Press, 1992); Alan Aldridge, *Religion in the Contemporary World* (Cambridge: Polity Press, 2000); Pippa Norris and Ronald Inglehart, *Sacred and Secular: Religion and Politics Worldwide* (New York: Cambridge University Press, 2004).

Sociologist José Casanova broke down the theory of secularization (according to which modernization causes secularization) into three sub-theories as follows: "(a) the theory of the institutional differentiation of the so-called secular spheres, such as state, economy, and science, from religious institutions and norms; (b) the theory of the progressive decline of religious beliefs and practices as a concomitant of levels of modernization; and (c) the theory of privatization of religion as a precondition of modern secular and democratic politics."[2] The three sub-theories are based on observations made in some Western European countries, but in the case of the United States, Casanova tells us, "by contrast, one finds a paradigmatic process of secular differentiation, which is not accompanied, however, either by a process of religious decline or by the confinement of religion to the private sphere. Processes of modernization and democratization in American society have often been accompanied by religious revivals."[3] The reverse of privatization is a religion turning public after a period of privatization or repression. This phenomenon, which is also referred to as "desecularization," characterizes Romania and other Central and Eastern European countries which, after 1989, have moved away from communist dictatorship.

Desecularization, a concept Peter Berger first introduced in 1999, was further clarified by Vyacheslav Karpov. According to Karpov, a distinction should be made between "desecularization proper and a much broader class of phenomena pertaining to religions' growth and expanding influence on societies."[4] Drawing on several sociologists of religion (Berger, Rodney Stark, Roger Finke, Grace Davie, but also Pitirim Sorokin), Karpov defines desecularization as counter-secularization: in other words, desecularization should not be mistaken for the natural growth of religions that involves peaks and valleys, but should be seen as a reaction against previous attempts at secularization. He also argues that secularization and desecularization possibly co-exist as complementary, rather than mutually exclusive, aspects of modern societies. One aspect of desecularization that is important in the case of Romania is "religion-related changes in society's substratum" (including the "reappearance of

---

2   José Casanova, "The Secular, Secularizations, Secularisms," in *Rethinking Secularism*, eds. Craig Calhoun, Mark Juergensmeyer and Jonathan Van Antwerpen (New York: Oxford University Press, 2011), 54; cf. also Idem, *Public Religions in the Modern World* (Chicago: Chicago University Press, 1994).
3   Casanova, "The Secular, Secularizations, Secularisms."
4   Vyacheslav Karpov, "Desecularization: A Conceptual Framework," *Journal of Church and State*, 52, no. 2 (2010): 232–70.

faith-related material structures, growing shares of religion-related goods in the overall economic market").

Although the Romanian Orthodox Church (ROC) has been the subject of increased scholarly attention, to date its financial and economic activities have remained understudied. Several factors account for this. Financial and economic activities have been seen as having only secondary importance to the ROC's life in post-communist times, the Romanian state has never compelled the church to fully disclose its assets, and the church has been reluctant to share information on this topic with the public. With a membership reaching 85% of the total population of 20 million, the ROC remains the country's dominant religious group. Its nine metropolitan sees (six of which are in Romania) include a total of 11,146 parishes in which 14,035 priests and deacons serve in 15,116 places of worship. To these we should add 631 monasteries and sketes with 8,059 monks and nuns, as well as 275 museums and 42 centers for the preservation and restoration of religious objects.[5] Whereas in communist times the ROC's political, social and economic presence in the lives of ordinary Romanians was negligible, after 1989 the church expanded its social and economic activities to an unprecedented degree, in many respects even surpassing its position pre-communism.

This article looks at two major themes connected to the financial and economic activities of the ROC before and after 2007, the year when Romania joined the European Union (EU). The article first presents the main sources of revenue and wealth of the ROC: subventions from the state, the restitution of assets confiscated by the communist authorities, donations collected from various groups and individuals, money obtained for services and religious artifacts offered to believers, and other revenue-generating activities. Second, the article discusses two instances in which the ROC has come under attack for the way it collects and uses money: the contributions it receives from the reserve fund of the government, and the church's efforts to finance the building in downtown Bucharest of a monumental national cathedral. The last section uses a test of secularization, based on the observations of José Casanova and Vyacheslav Karpov, to measure if and how much Romania has secularized, especially in light of the economic and financial aspects of church activity presented in this article. Before delving into these two main themes, the article provides a brief historical examination that explains state control over church assets,

---

5   Cornel Mihalache, "Fabrica de bani: Biserica Ortodoxă Română. Averea și afacerile BOR," TVR1 documentary (December 3, 2013), https://www.youtube.com/watch?v=sjRX70d-vks, accessed on October 13, 2020.

church-state relations during pre-communist, communist and post-communist times, as well as the church's views on the capitalist market economy and its own involvement in revenue-generating activities.

Church finances before and after communism

Several major historical markers have impacted church economic activities during the past two centuries. As the denomination of the tolerated Romanian ethnic group, the Orthodox Church in Transylvania had only very limited maneuvering space for collecting revenues and increasing its wealth, but the situation in Romania's other territories was quite different, the Orthodox Church having vast resources and assets. Starting in 1834 the revenues of the Orthodox Church in Moldova and Wallachia were collected centrally, thus becoming known to state officials for the first time. In 1859 church revenues represented 42% of all revenues collected by the Wallachian government, and 10% to 20% of those gathered by the Moldovan government. In 1861, the land owned by Orthodox monasteries represented a quarter of the entire Romanian territory (the Principalities of Wallachia and Moldova became known as Romania in 1861). Two years later the state nationalized most church land and assets, while continuing to include church revenues into the national budget. The government, not the church, decided how those revenues were to be used. Therefore, in 1866 only one-third of confiscated church assets, which represented one-quarter of all revenues to the public budget, were directed toward church activities.[6]

After the aggressive nationalization campaign left the church destitute by requisitioning most of its assets, state officials agreed to return some land to the church and to contribute funds for the wages and pensions of the clergy and bursaries to theology seminary students. This help, however, came with a downside. The clergy's income dropped as state and church contributions towards salaries could not match pre-nationalization levels. As the main financier of church activity, the state also took upon itself to reduce the number of clergy who received remuneration, and to introduce reforms that subordinated the church to the state in all respects. At the beginning of the 20th century, therefore, the Orthodox Church had access to only minuscule land plots that could allow it to derive income from agriculture. At the same time, the state covered signifi-

---

6   Iuliana Conovici (ed), *Organizațiile cu profil religios angajate în economia socială în România* (București: Institutul de Economie Socială, 2013), 37.

cant church expenses for salaries and the maintenance of places of worship—as compensation for the wealth lost through nationalization. The church could meet only 3% of its expenses, so state subsidies were vital for its survival.[7]

The communist regime further restricted church activities and subjected all denominations to persecution after World War II. In 1950, Orthodox monasteries owned 18,400 hectares of agricultural land, 20,500 hectares of forest, animals, beehives, two publishing presses, and workshops for weaving and making rugs, wine, paintings, sculptures, and crosses.[8] These properties barely allowed the church to survive financially. Deprived of its pre-communist right to engage in charitable activities, the church used its modest revenue to maintain its churches and monasteries, and supplement the meager income of its clergy, whose role in communities was greatly diminished by the self-avowed atheistic communist state. Two communist-era developments are relevant for this discussion. The first refers to the communist nationalization of church assets, through which the Orthodox Church lost some of its assets to the communist government but gained Greek Catholic land and buildings when that church was disbanded in 1948. The ROC increased its wealth but became responsible for maintaining the newly acquired buildings. These transfers' uncertain ownership status complicated the property restitution program launched in post-communist times.

Second, inspired equally by his socialist convictions and by pragmatic calculations about the church's survival under extremely harsh repression, Patriarch Justinian Marina (1948–1977) introduced reforms to make monasteries self-sufficient and the church less financially dependent on communist authorities. His plans, however, were justified by a doctrine he called "social apostolate," that eventually brought the church even more firmly under the control of the communist state. According to this doctrine, "the church was subservient to the state as the 'servant church of the people', while the state assured religious liberty."[9] Marina's pact of agreement, subordination and collaboration with the self-avowed atheistic communist authorities managed to partially shield the ROC from the anticlerical repressive campaigns of the early decades of communist rule and even placed the church in a privileged position compared to other religious groups. At the same time, it also largely

---

7   Ibid., 43.
8   Ibid., 45.
9   Lucian N. Leustean, *Orthodoxy and the Cold War: Religion and Political Power in Romania, 1947–65* (London: Palgrave Macmillan, 2009), 74.

maintained the ROC's heavy financial dependence on the state, whose support the church looked for when seeking to cover the clergy's salaries and pensions, to restore places of worship deemed of historical value, and to cover expenses related to the administration of church affairs. This dependence was retained almost unchanged by the other communist-era patriarchs, Iustinian Moisescu (1977–1986) and Teoctist Arapasu (1986–2007). The church's collaboration with the dictatorial governments in exchange of a privileged status was dubbed 'Byzantinism.'[10]

Immediately after 1989, the ROC asked the Romanian state to continue to contribute towards clergy salaries and wages, but to stop interfering in its internal organization and activities. Over time, it significantly expanded its social and economic activities, benefiting from a favorable legislative framework and tax-exemption status. Governmental Decisions 122 and 373 of 1992 as well as Law 142 of 1999 pledged state contributions toward the salaries of priests and laypeople involved in church activities, including teachers of religion classes offered in public schools.[11] Law 103 of 1992 gave religious denominations exclusive rights to produce and sell religious objects like chalices, icons, candles, religious vestments, bibles and other religious books, and offered tax exemptions for these activities.[12] Law 345 of 2002 granted the ROC tax exemptions for its land, churches and other buildings, permits to build in urban areas, and electricity to heat its places of worship.[13] The most important post-communist piece of legislation defining relations between the state and the recognized denominations, Law 489 of 2006, allowed denominations to fund their work from taxes, donations and contributions received from

---

10 Olivier Gillet, *Les Balkans: Religions et nationalisme* (Brussels: Éditions Ousia, 2001), 77.
11 "Hotararea nr. 122 privind unele măsuri legate de salarizarea clerului și a altor categorii de personal al cultelor," *Monitorul Oficial*, no. 49, March 24, 1992, http://legislatie.just.ro/Public/DetaliiDocument/2430; "Hotararea nr. 373 din 3 iulie 1992 privind salarizarea clerului și a altor categorii de personal al cultelor," *Monitorul Oficial*, 167, July 17, 1992, http://legislatie.just.ro/Public/DetaliiDocument/2656; "Legea nr. 142/1999 privind sprijinul statului pentru salarizarea clerului," *Monitorul Oficial*, 361, July 27, 1999, http://www.dreptonline.ro/legislatie/legea_salarizare_cler.php, all accessed on May 8, 2020.
12 "Legea nr. 103/1992 dreptul exclusiv al cultelor religioase pentru producerea obiectelor de cult," *Monitorul Oficial*, no. 244, October, 1, 1992, https://legeaz.net/text-integral/legea-103-1992-dreptul-exclusiv-al-cultelor-religioase-producerea-obiectelor-de-cult, accessed on May 8, 2020.
13 "Legea nr. 345/2002 privind taxa pe valoarea adăugată," *Monitorul Oficial*, 371, June 1, 2002, http://www.cdep.ro/pls/legis/legis_pck.htp_act_text?idt=35518, accessed on May 8, 2020.

the faithful for baptism, marriage, consecration, and funeral services.[14] And Governmental Emergency Ordinance 155 of 2008 raised the salaries of the priests to levels comparable to pre-university teachers.[15]

This legislative framework was meant to make the ROC, and the other religious denominations present in Romania, financially able to fund an ever-growing number of social programs and charities. In 2015, the press reported that the ROC ran 785 social institutions and programs, including 158 canteens and bread shops, 51 medical and dentistry cabinets and pharmacies, 123 daycare centers, kindergartens and after-school programs for children, 63 education centers, 58 day and home-care centers for the elderly, 64 community and family centers, 94 information, counseling and resource centers, 1 adult education facility, 21 shelters for battered women and the homeless, as well as 21 summer camps.[16] In addition, the ROC has its own publishing houses, radio and television stations (Trinitas), pilgrimage travel agency (Basilica Travel), seminaries and theological schools at the pre-university and university levels. Its monasteries are renowned sites of pilgrimage, good food and wine, and spiritual retreat.

Note that the ROC has kept silent on whether its involvement in the market economy and profit-making activities, either as an institution or with respect to the believers as individuals, is in tune with church dogma and tradition. That the church has implicitly embraced private enterprise can be gathered from its revenue-generating initiatives, which cover its operating expenses, finance its philanthropic work, and lead its constituency to its ultimate spiritual goal (salvation of souls). Capitalist consumerism might be more acceptable because the ROC "regards the organized materialism of communist states as a more frightening enemy than the unorganized materialism of capitalist societies, since the former is more exclusive and more intolerant toward spiritual independence."[17]

---

14 "Legea nr. 489/2006 privind libertatea religioasă și regimul general al cultelor," *Monitorul Oficial*, no. 11, January 8, 2007, https://www.crestinism-ortodox.ro/TEXTE/LegeaCultelor-Nr489-2006.pdf, accessed on May 8, 2020. See also Conovici, *Organizatiile cu profil religios*, 62–3.
15 "OUG nr. 155/2008 pentru modificarea Legii nr. 142/1999 privind sprijinul statului pentru salarizarea clerului," *Monitorul Oficial*, no. 778, November 20, 2008, http://www.dreptonline.ro/legislatie/oug_modificare_sprijinul_statului_sa larizarea_clerului_155_2008.php, accessed on May 8, 2020.
16 Andrei Luca Popescu, "Sfintele afaceri ale Bisericii Ortodoxe," *Gândul*, August 18, 2015, http://www.gandul.info/stiri/sfintele-afaceri-ale-bisericii-ortodoxe-topul-celor-mai-bogate-eparhii-ale-bor-si-ce-profituri-au-declarat-la-finante-14679822, accessed on November 21, 2017.
17 Cătălin Raiu, Ortodoxie, postcomunism și neoliberalism: o critică teologico-politică (București: Editura Curtea Veche, 2012), 126.

At the same time, the ROC has explicitly showed support for Western liberal multi-party democracy. This was demonstrated by Decision no. 1676 of 2008 of the ROC national leadership, the Holy Synod, which explicitly promised that the church will contribute "to the defense of democracy, liberty, faith in God, the independence and integrity of the Fatherland, rejecting any form of totalitarian and atheist communism, as well as any form of extremism."[18]

ROC's sources of wealth

The ROC's lack of transparency regarding its financial transactions, economic activities, and accounting practices raised concerns that the church has amassed considerable wealth after 1989, and prompted journalists to nickname it the "Godporation"—God's corporation.[19] Critics point to the tax exemptions the church enjoys and the frequent hefty subsidies it receives from the state to argue for an end to these benefits, especially since cash-strapped post-communist governments have had to drastically cut social programs benefiting young families with children, the elderly, and disadvantaged social groups. The conspicuous consumption and lavish lifestyle of some of the Orthodox leaders, whose penchant for expensive watches and luxury cars is insatiable, seem to suggest that the ROC directs enormous financial resources to its own material wellbeing more than to charitable projects. The church, in turn, has responded to such criticisms by enumerating the many orphanages, hospitals, medical and dentistry clinics, and pilgrimage centers that it supports financially, and the expensive maintenance costs of its numerous places of worship, many of them declared inestimable historical and architectural monuments.

The ROC submits annual reports to the Ministry of Finance that are not readily available to the public and that grossly underestimate church revenues, because not all received donations and service fees are recorded in the church's books. Accounting practices are outdated and opaque, according to church insiders. In the case of monasteries and

---

18 "Hotărârea Sfântului Sinod, nr. 1676 din 5–7 martie 2008", http://patriarhia.ro/hotararea-sfantului-sinod-nr-1676-din-5-7-martie-2008-2837.html, accessed on May 8, 2020.
19 Adriana Stanca, "Godporația. Cu câți bani a 'sponsorizat' Biserica fostul președinte al Consiliului Județean Mehedinți, Adrian Duicu," *Gândul*, October 30, 2014, http://www.gandul.info/stiri/godporatia-cu-cati-bani-a-sponsorizat-biserica-fostul-presedinte-al-consiliului-judetean-mehedinti-adrian-duicu-13479491, accessed on November 17, 2017.

donations made under the table by individuals and political parties, accounting practices are simply non-existent, as these proceedings are often never reported to the national church leader or the revenue authorities. Thus, "monasteries are the personal banks of local bishops" and "the [unreported] 'black money' are left at the discretion of the bishop, who must cover ... court expenses [and] political favors."[20] The ROC's annual revenues were estimated at 50 million euros in 2008, 60 million euros in 2010, and 65 million euros in 2014.[21] According to a 2018 communique, Vasile Bănescu, the official ROC spokesperson, said that "over the past 10 years, the Romanian Orthodox Church spent 150 million Euros on social and charitable activities, and last year [alone] over 24 million Euros."[22] These figures strongly contradict the allegations of organizations like Stop State Funding for Churches (Opriti Finantarea Cultelor Religioase) that the ROC allocates only a mere 2.5% of the subsidies it receives from the state to charitable activities.[23] Allegations that the total wealth of the Orthodox Church is much larger, reaching 3 billion euros in 2007, have not been substantiated yet.[24]

Since 1989 the ROC has derived revenue from several different sources: 1) state subsidies for church activities and operating funds, 2) assets acquired through the restitution of property abusively confiscated by the communist regime, 3) donations of land, money, goods and services received from individuals and groups, 4) fees for services performed for believers or communities, and 5) the production and selling of various religious artifacts. Few official numbers are available to describe each of these activities with accuracy. The discussion below relies on a combination of governmental reports, church statements, and

---

20 Gabriel Mascas, quoted in Mihalache, "Fabrica de bani."
21 Alex Nedea, *Să fie primit! Preoții fac afaceri personale din bani publici*, documentary, February 2, 2014, http://morometia.ro/ofcr/afaceri/investigatie-sa-fie-primit/, accessed on October 29, 2015; "Cum s-au mișcat banii Bisericii Ortodoxe Române în anul 2014," Forbes Romania, July 8, 2015, http://www.forbes.ro/cum-s-au-miscat-banii-bisericii-ortodoxe-romane-anul-2014-41667, accessed on May 8, 2020.
22 "Bănescu: Ministrul Finanțelor a apreciat acțiunile filantropice ale Bisericiiș; perspectiva preluată în presă—falsă," Agerpres, 12 February 2018, https://www.agerpres.ro/culte/2018/02/12/banescu-ministrul-finantelor-a-apreciat-actiunile-filantropice-ale-bisericii-perspectiva-preluata-in-presa-falsa—53357, accessed on October 11, 2020.
23 "Afaceri și binefaceri: BOR vs ONG," Opriți Finanțarea Cultelor Religioase, February 27, 2014, http://morometia.ro/ofcr/investigatii/afaceri-si-binefaceri-bor-vs-ong/, accessed on October 29, 2015.
24 Mihalache, "Fabrica de bani."

news articles, but it should be recognized that all of them paint only the most general contour of the ROC's wealth.

The contributions of successive post-communist governments to the ROC and other religious groups are perceived by secular groups as either wasteful of resources that could be used for much-needed social programs or unjustified, given the denominations' vast wealth and tax-exemption status. After 1989, the national government (through the State Secretariat for Religious Affairs), the county and local councils, and most public utility companies, have granted subsidies to denominations, especially the majority church. Subsidies increased sharply in electoral years, when parties forming the government (and those representing the opposition) sought support for their candidates from priests and bishops able to sway voter preferences. According to a documentary, the ROC received ever growing state subsidies in electoral years: USD 4.7 million in 1992 from Prime Minister Teodor Stolojan, USD 12 million in 1996 from Nicolae Vacaroiu, USD 25 million in 2000 from Mugur Isarescu, USD 32 million in 2000 from Adrian Nastase, and USD 121 million in 2008 from Calin Popescu Tariceanu.[25] State subsidies to all religions amount to only 0.2% of the national budget and are often obtained only after submitting documented requests, but they continue to come under attack from secular groups that think Romania should emulate France and finance no religious group.[26] Church representatives argue that state subsidies are justified, since they represent a fraction of the taxes paid by the Romanian citizens, who are Orthodox in their vast majority.[27]

State subsidies to the ROC have been allocated to two main destinations: the salaries and pensions of church members, and the maintenance and construction of places of worship. First, the state covers 60% of the salaries of diocesan priests, and 80% in the case of priests serving in poor rural communities. The remainder represents contributions from the ROC, mostly in the form of donations and service fees received from the faithful. State contributions to clergy salaries amount monthly to 250 to 450 euros for priests, 1,400 euros for bishops, 1,700 euros for metropolitans, and 1,800 euros for the patriarch.[28] The state finances a limited

---

25 Nedea, *Să fie primit!*
26 Dan Brumar, "Biserica Ortodoxă pune condiții pentru a accepta să fie impozitată", *Click.ro*, August 27, 2015, http://www.click.ro/news/national/biserica-ortodoxa-pune-conditii-pentru-accepta-sa-fie-impozitata, accessed on October 22, 2015.
27 Bogdan Ivanov, cited in Mihalache, "Fabrica de bani."
28 The average monthly wage was 515 euros in 2017, and 398 euros in 2014. State contributions to the patriarch's salary amount to half the salary of the Romanian prime minister. See "Average Salary in European Union 2017," *Reinis Fischer*, April

number of religious leadership positions: one patriarch, one head rabbi, one head imam, ten metropolitans, 13 archbishops, 31 bishops, and 23 auxiliary bishops.[29] Additional public funds are allocated for the salaries of monastery leaders, diocesan councilors, and church administrators. The income tax for clergy members reaches 31% of their combined state and church salaries, meaning that state subsidies cover only 29% to 49% of salaries. The state also pays a part of the salaries of 15,327 ministers of various religious denominations, 70% of whom are Orthodox, according to Law 284/2010. It also covers in full the wages of chaplains working in prisons and for the police, army and intelligence services, as well as the salaries of the 7,700 teachers of religion in public schools and 100 professors teaching in ten Faculties of Orthodox Theology.[30] Religion classes have been offered in schools since the early 1990s.[31]

Second, the ROC has also received considerable state funds for the maintenance of old and the construction of new places of worship. Some of these old buildings are seen as having historical and national importance and are too expensive for the church to maintain by itself, given the delicate restoration work needed to consolidate their structure and repair their murals. In 2014, for example, government agencies at all levels allocated to the ROC some 24 million euros, divided equally for maintaining Orthodox churches and monasteries and building the national cathedral in Bucharest (see below). As 2014 was an electoral year, national budget contributions to the ROC, a powerful political player that few electoral candidates can ignore, were almost four times larger than in 2013.[32] Local government bodies also make regular contributions toward the maintenance of diocesan churches, for reasons related to the spiritual welfare of the local community more than the historical or architectural value of these places of worship.

Demands for restitution of property confiscated by the communist regime were raised immediately after the December 1989 regime change.

22, 2017, https://www.reinisfischer.com/average-salary-european-union-2017, accessed on November 17, 2017.
29 APADOR-CH, *Stat și religii în România—o relație transparentă?* (București: Asociația pentru Apărarea Drepturilor Omului în România—Comitetul Helsinki, 2008), 20, https://archive.org/details/Samsara.2011.BRRip.XviD.AC3.RoSubbed PlayXD, accessed on October 30, 2017.
30 Tiberiu M. Pana, "Studiu de caz: Despre pomenile guvernamentale și preacucernicii beneficiari ai acestora," *Contributors.ro*, October 15, 2014, http://www.contributors.ro/editorial/studiu-de-caz-despre-pomenile-guvernamentale-si-preac ucernicii-lor-beneficiari-2/, accessed on October 29, 2015.
31 Lavinia Stan and Lucian Turcescu, "Religious Education in Romania," *Communist and Post-Communist Studies*, 38 (2005): 381–401.
32 Popescu, "Sfintele afaceri ale Bisericii Ortodoxe."

Religious representatives and former individual property owners have argued that the new Romanian state could hardly ignore the fundamental right to property, as its communist predecessor did with impunity. The post-communist restitution program affected the ROC in two major ways. On the one hand, the ROC was asked to return the Transylvanian chapels, churches, cemeteries, and land plots it gained access to or ownership over in 1948, when the communists disbanded the Greek Catholic Church and unilaterally rescinded the Concordat with the Vatican. In a protracted process during which the state retreated to the position of a mere mediator between the two denominations, the ROC refused to relinquish most of these assets, thus forcing many Greek Catholic communities to erect new village churches for their own use. The Orthodox Church explained its refusal by reminding the public that many of the Greek Catholic churches slated for restitution had been confiscated from the Orthodox in 1700.[33]

On the other hand, the ROC urged successive governments to return its assets that were confiscated during communist and even pre-communist times. Most important among those was the land the church lost through nationalization in the mid-19th century (see above). By 2011, the ROC reportedly owned 70,000 hectares of forest and 40,000 hectares of agricultural land, whose combined value reached 420 million euros.[34] At the same time, the church has obtained hundreds of buildings through restitution. Whenever possible, the state transferred the ownership of these buildings to the ROC. In other cases, the government has allowed the church to use state-owned hotels, spas, apartment blocs, farms, and schools. Whether the church could make money out of these assets remains unclear.

These assets and funds received from the state have been supplemented by donations of money, land or consumer goods from individual believers, firms, organizations, and political parties. There are no estimates for most of these donations, and they do not seem to be recorded systematically anywhere. Individuals donate to the ROC mostly during major religious celebrations (Christmas and Easter) or to mark significant life events (the welcoming of a child, baptism, marriage or death). Church representatives have reported that many low and medium income families contribute small sums of money on a regular basis, but believers also give items such as carpets, food, cars, and consumer products to their

---

33 Lavinia Stan and Lucian Turcescu, *Religion and Politics in Post-Communist Romania* (New York: Oxford University Press, 2007).
34 Mihalache, "Fabrica de bani."

priests or help the church to complete various construction and cleaning projects.[35] In 2009, almost one in three taxpayers donated up to 2% of their income tax to the ROC, by filling in a special form. That year, 33% of all Romanians declared that they manifested their civic spirit by making donations to the church.[36] Businessmen, former mayors and politicians have donated lavishly toward the construction of new churches or the painting of old ones.[37]

In addition, the ROC's priests receive payment for the many services they offer to believers: baptism, marriage and death ceremonies; the blessing of homes, cars, plots of land, large animals, tractors, and new businesses; land and user fees for cemetery plots; and pilgrimages to religious sites in Romania and abroad. While believers sometimes complain that these fees are rather high and thus difficult to pay by low-income families, priests in small and aging localities are unable to collect significant funds when such services are very few and the community is poor. Maybe this is the reason why some of these transactions are not recorded properly, and believers do not receive receipts for the money they give to the priest.

In contrast to the fixed fees imposed in Roman Catholic churches in Romania after 2010, each Orthodox priest can charge as much as he wants for these services, and as such there is great fee disparity among ROC dioceses, because the Patriarchate refuses to impose official fees and leaves it to the markets to determine it. In Bucharest, marriage ceremonies cost between 50 and 330 euros, whereas baptism costs around 135 euros, but prices are lower in smaller towns and villages.[38] Some priests accept no money for such services, others suggest a minimum sum, and still others would not perform the ceremony unless they collect the fee first. Fees for

---

35 "Catedrala Mantuirii Neamului— oamenii sărăraci și bătrânii, cei mai conștiincioși donatori," *Ziare.com*, February 13, 2014, http://www.ziare.com/social/biserica/catedrala-mantuirii-neamului-oamenii-saraci-si-batranii-cei-mai-constiinciosi-donatori-1282530, accessed on October 29, 2017.
36 Ana Batca, "Cum reușește Biserica să atragă donații de la români," *Evenimentul Zilei*, May 4, 2010, http://ziarero.antena3.ro/articol.php?id=1272956498, accessed on November 15, 2017.
37 Mihaela Floroiu and Mirela Cimpoi, "Moda sfinților politicieni," *Ziare.ro*, March 15, 2008, http://ziarero.antena3.ro/articol.php?id=1205561727, accessed on October 29, 2015; and Adrian N. Paunescu, "Cele mai neobișnuite picturi din bisericile românești," *Atlas Geografic*, September 2, 2015, http://atlas-geografic.net/cele-mai-neobisnuite-picturi-din-bisericile-romanesti/, accessed on October 29, 2015.
38 Mihaela Stoica, "Cât dă nașul la BISERICĂ la nuntă și la botez: chitanțierul neoficial al preoților din București, din marile orașe și de la țară," *Gândul*, October 19, 2013, http://www.gandul.info/stiri/cat-da-nasul-la-biserica-la-nunta-si-la-botez-chitantierul-neoficial-al-preotilor-din-bucuresti-din-marile-orase-si-de-la-tara-11526172, accessed on October 29, 2015.

blessing ceremonies are even less regulated and differ significantly from village to town. In the Constanta county, for example, the blessing of a car reportedly costs on average some 15 euros, and that of a house 12 euros.[39]

In the case of cemeteries, the ROC has often persuaded local government bodies to transfer them to it or to give it exclusive rights to perform funerary services in the village cemetery, if ownership transfer was not possible. New Orthodox cemeteries have opened after 1989 on land donated to the church by the local government. The ROC charges user fees even in those cases, although civil society groups argue that such fees are unnecessary and immoral. In a much talked about case, a funerary firm connected to the Patriarchate obtained exclusive rights to operate in two cemeteries located in a village at the outskirts of Bucharest. Before the firm established control over the cemetery the villagers could bury their relatives themselves, but afterwards the firm asked for around 250 euros per burial.[40] The average monthly wage in Romania was about 398 euros in 2014.[41] Fearful of losing revenue, the ROC has bitterly contested Law 102 of 2014, which facilitated the opening of private cemeteries, granted non-Christian cemeteries additional privileges, and guaranteed the right to cremation and burial without a priest. It is still too early to say whether the church's fears were justified.

Like in other parts of the world, pilgrimages have become extremely popular in post-communist Romania, with Orthodox believers visiting renowned monasteries in the country, as well as sites of interest abroad. Most pilgrims are devout women, with many of them being young or middle-aged. The most popular pilgrimage in Romania is the one to the relics of Saint Parascheva in Iasi, Moldova, which brings between 350,000 and 500,000 people to the city each year. Several monasteries are famed centers of pilgrimage where Romanians spend their holidays in tranquility. In Putna, Agapia, Varatec, Neamt, Sambata de Jos, and Tismana the church maintains impressive hotels and inns where pilgrims can spend the night

---

39   Maria Radu, "BOR și-a updatat lista de prețuri pentru rugăciuni la modă", *Adevărul*, July 24, 2013, http://muntenia-news.ro/national/exclusiv-bor-si-a-updatat-lista-de-preturi-pentru-rugaciuni-la-moda-cat-costa-sfintirea-masinii-si-a-casei-preot-o-suma-modica-dar-zece/, accessed on October 29, 2015. See "Cât costă taxa cununie religioasă ăn anul 2020?" *Revista Nunta*, June 24, 2020, https://revista nunta.ro/taxa-cununie-religioasa/, accessed on October 11, 2020

40   "Patriarhia Română, monopol pe înmormântări," *Ziare.com*, March 14, 2014, http://www.ziare.com/social/biserica/patriarhia-romana-monopol-pe-inmorma ntari-cimitire-in-care-nu-ai-voie-sa-ti-ingropi-mortul-decat-cu-firmele-bor-1287841, accessed on November 15, 2017.

41   See "Average Salary in European Union 2017."

and share a meal. None of these tourist units report annual revenues independently to the Ministry, and some of them are in archbishoprics that never submit any financial reports. Since not all pilgrims are required to pay for lodging or meals and prices are often decided on an ad-hoc basis, it is difficult to estimate total revenues from these tourist activities.

The ROC's travel agency, Basilica Travel, is controlled by the Patriarchate and offers local and international tours in the company of specialized Orthodox guides, usually graduates of the Faculty of Orthodox Theology. In 2014 Basilica Travel reported a profit of 115,000 euros.[42] Competition between Basilica and other travel agencies remains fierce. Orthodox priests also organize trips without the knowledge of Basilica representatives, but the Patriarchate introduced regulations trying to curb such activities over which it has no control. Only 80% of these priests are officially accredited to organize such trips. Some 40,000 Romanians visit Israel every year, of whom 25,000 with Basilica Travel. Groups travelling with Basilica are allegedly charged 10% more than other tour operators charge.[43]

The ROC also derives revenue from producing and selling books, religious calendars, pamphlets, candles, icons, liturgical wine, and incense to believers, and priestly attire to the clergy. Since 2013, some of these artifacts can be ordered on the website of the Patriarchate, but most believers buy them in churches, monasteries or the specialized stores of the ROC located in big cities.[44] According to Law 103 of 1992 the church has exclusive rights to produce religious artifacts, but in practice authorities do not enforce this monopoly and the church loses revenue to competitor profit-making firms. For example, the ROC produces candles and then sells them to believers who attend mass or ask for various ceremonies. It is customary for Orthodox believers to light candles during mass, when they visit the church to commemorate their loved ones, and when they solicit baptism, marriage or funeral services. The price for candles pro-

---

42   Popescu, "Sfintele afaceri ale Bisericii Ortodoxe."
43   Economica, "Veniturile agenției de pelerinaj, folosite pentru activitățile sociale ale BOR," *Economica.net*, November 13, 2013, http://www.economica.net/replica-patriarhiei-veniturile-agentiei-de-pelerinaj-folosite-pentru-activitatile-sociale-ale-bor_66652.html#ixzz3pKmXi1qC, accessed on October 21, 2015.
44   Flavia Dragan, "Cruci de vânzare, binecuvântate de Patriarhul Daniel. Biserica Ortodoxă și-a lansat un magazin virtual," *Romania Liberă*, January 25, 2013, http://www.romanialibera.ro/actualitate/eveniment/cruci-de-vanzare—binecuvantate-de-patriarhul-daniel--biserica-ortodoxa-si-a-lansat-un-magazin-virtual-291416, accessed on October 29, 2015.

duced by the ROC is often 2.5 times higher than the price at which metropolitans offer them to dioceses. This ensures a hefty profit for the Orthodox leadership, which claims to invest it in charity.

The church patronizes several revenue-generating enterprises that produce wool, wine, brandy, or timber, on which there is no information other than the church's insistent claims that all these activities fund charity. Investigative journalists have also documented church involvement in profit-making firms. For example, Praxis, a company set up by the Craiova Archbishopric, has 12% of all shares in the Elcomex energy distribution firm. Church representatives admitted that Praxis was created in the hope of bringing additional funds for the organization of pilgrimages and for a local radio station broadcasting religious programs. In addition, through trusted intermediaries, the bishops allegedly control local firms that do not list the ROC as an official partner, although they give the church access to additional unaccounted funds. Because of the ROC's tremendous influence on the political elite, state officials and the general population, few if any audits have ever focused on the financial transactions and economic activities of the church. Not all metropolitanates and archbishoprics submit data to the Ministry of Finance on an annual basis, and they are not subject to the penalties received by commercial firms in that situation. Critics have questioned the ROC's involvement in profit-making activities while it enjoys tax-exempt status, calling for its privileges to be revoked.[45]

Controversies

In two notable instances the ROC has come under attack for the way it obtained and used funds. First are the recurrent public debates revolving around the contributions received by the ROC from the special reserve fund placed at the discretion of the prime minister. Second, the public criticism surrounding the church's sustained efforts to finance the building of a monumental national cathedral in downtown Bucharest which would integrate large pilgrimage and healthcare centers.

The Government Reserve Fund

Since 1989, a constant in Romanian politics has been the willingness of prime ministers of all ideological colors to make substantial payments to the ROC, in addition to the subsidies the state offers annually to all reli-

---

45   Mihalache, "Fabrica de bani."

gious groups through the State Secretariat for Religious Affairs. Allocations from the reserve fund are made through government decisions published in the state gazette. Although they are in this sense transparent, to date no systematic analysis of reserve fund allocations has been conducted, mainly because the large number of decisions precludes the exact identification of resolutions on allocations to the ROC, in the absence of a search engine. For example, in 2007 almost 18.6 million euros were allocated to the ROC through government decisions. The money covered the organization of an ecumenical meeting, the state funeral of Patriarch Teoctist, the ceremonies connected to the installation of Patriarch Daniel, as well as the maintenance and building of churches.[46] Note that the ROC accessed only 3% of the reserve fund in 2007.[47]

Contributions to the ROC from the government reserve fund remain controversial for several reasons. First, according to the legislation the reserve fund is to be used for situations of emergencies that cannot be anticipated before the start of the fiscal year, and thus cannot be included in the national budget, which is presented for approval to parliament. Nevertheless, the maintenance and constructions of churches, and the organization of religious events could hardly be seen as emergency cases when such projects have been ongoing or known for some time. A related point is that the national budget needs the approval of both chambers of parliament, whereas governmental decisions need only the approval of the cabinet. Decisions are passed with far fewer support votes than laws and are less democratic, because they completely exclude the opposition from voicing an opinion on such allocations. They require none of the written motivations that laws do, and as such are often seen as directing money to questionable destinations in times of budgetary constraints.

Second, there are concerns about undue influence on the part of the church over government officials, and on the part of the government over the church. Indeed, most of these reserve fund allocations are hastily decided either at the end of the fiscal year or during the months leading to elections. Such hurried allocations could be interpreted in two ways. On the one hand, they could reflect the pressure exerted by ROC leaders over the prime minister and the government to disburse additional funds through a mechanism that generally ignores the need for proportionality between the majority and minority religions. On the other hand, they

---

46   APADOR-CH, *Stat și religii în România*.
47   Curtea de Conturi a României, *Raport public pe anul 2008*, http://www.curtea deconturi.ro/Publicatii/RPA2008(MO).pdf, accessed on November 15, 2017.

could amount to bribes given by the political parties forming the government to the powerful ROC, whose priests could encourage voters to cast ballots in favor of select candidates. That is because most fund allocations to ROC are made in the months leading to elections. Both situations reflect the tight relationship between the majority denomination and the political elite.

Third, critics have pointed out that overall the ROC has received more funds than what its share of the population entitles it to (that is, around 85%). This preference for the majority church has come at the detriment of religious minorities and has augmented the already unbalanced allocation of public funds through the State Secretariat, whose leaders until recently were always graduates of the Faculty of Orthodox Theology. Note that the vast majority of disbursements from the government reserve fund lack transparency and accountability and are decided by the cabinet in isolation from and with no consultation with other political parties and civil society members. Disbursements from the reserve funds of the county and local councils are equally lacking in transparency, although sometimes they are accompanied by a written rationale.[48]

The National Cathedral

The building of a national cathedral, considered a priority since the 1990s, has prompted the ROC to step up its efforts to generate revenue, collect donations, and receive state subsidies. From the start, the project has elicited vigorous public debates, pitting the church against secular groups. For the church, the new cathedral seems to symbolize "the central place Orthodoxy occupies in the heart and mind of the nation," to reflect "religious rebirth, Orthodox morality and a special church-state partnership," and to represent "a symbolic compensation for the failure of politicians to grant the Orthodox Church national church status" immediately after the collapse of the communist regime. Secular groups, by contrast, have described the cathedral as "a symbol of intolerance, clericalism, a waste of resources.[49] After numerous delays in acquiring the necessary building permits, considering several feasible locations in downtown Bucharest, and examining several possible designs, the church began construction in 2011. Located in proximity to the House of the People, a grandiose construction erected by communist dictator Nicolae Ceausescu that now houses the Romanian Parliament, the cathedral is part of a larger complex

---

48   APADOR-CH, Stat şi religii în România.
49   Lavinia Stan and Lucian Turcescu, "Politics, National Symbols and the Romanian Orthodox Cathedral," *Europe-Asia-Studies*, 58, no. 7 (2006), 1119–39.

that will include medical clinics and a pilgrimage center. The pharaonic cathedral is designed to be larger than all other Romanian Orthodox churches and taller than the House of the People. It was hoped that its construction would have been finalized by 2018, the year that will mark the 100th anniversary of the establishment of Greater Romania, but at the time of this writing in 2020, the construction is still ongoing although a symbolic inauguration did take place in 2018.

The costs were initially estimated at 100 million euros, to be covered equally by the ROC and the government, according to a 2007 proposal of the Senate. That proposal was rejected by the Chamber of Deputies, but the government has still contributed significant sums to the building project by adopting a series of government decisions. By 2015 the estimated costs had dropped to 80 million euros, and the state's financial contribution continued to remain undisclosed to the public. That year, the State Secretariat allocated 5.6 million euros to the construction. That was not the only public contribution, since several payments have been made from the reserve fund, several county councils and mayors' offices have also offered money, and the Bucharest city hall donated the 11 hectares of land on which the construction stands.[50]

Well before the construction site was opened, the ROC started to aggressively advertise the project and insistently ask for donations and contributions. After the ROC encouraged Romanians to donate part of their taxes to the cathedral, the latest initiative to collect money for the building site is the "official candle," which is inscribed with a text that specifically mentions the cathedral. Funds directed toward the cathedral account for a significant percentage of the ROC's revenues, perhaps surpassing the total value of its charitable activities. While the cathedral is the latest and the largest, it is not the only construction project that has been financed by the ROC since 1989. According to reports, hundreds of Orthodox churches have been constructed during the last 25 years with the help of state subsidies and donations from believers. Thus, in 2013 Romania had far more Orthodox churches than schools and hospitals: 18,300 compared to 4,700 and 425, respectively.[51]

---

50 Narcisa Balaban, "Senatorii au aprobat finanțarea pentru Catedrala Mântuirii Neamului", *Lumina*, September 5, 2007, http://ziarullumina.ro/senatorii-au-aprobat-finantarea-pentru-catedrala-mantuirii-neamului-65349.html, accessed on November 3, 2015.

51 Daniel Guta, "România, lăsată în plata Domnului. Ne închinăm pentru sănătate și educație: 18.300 de biserici, 4.700 de școli și 425 de spitale", *Adevărul*, February 5, 2015, http://adevarul.ro/news/societate/romania-lasata-plata-domnului-inchinam-sanatate-educatie-18300-biserici-4700-scoli-425-spitale-1_54d338d5448e03c0fd4cb7c5/index.html, accessed on November 3, 2015.

Church finances and secularization

If we apply the institutional differentiation sub-theory of secularization to Romania, we notice that a differentiation of secular spheres from religious institutions and norms began in the 19th century, continued through the 20th century, especially during the communist period, and is present to this day as a continuing reality. However, when considering the public funding of religion by the state either directly or indirectly, one can conclude that economically at least there has not been much separation. This funding is directed one way, that is, from the state to the church and not vice-versa. But the level of funding the state spends on religious institutions is significant, as we saw, and it includes a large portion of the salaries of most priests, the construction of new churches and the maintenance of the historic ones, paying the salaries of the teachers of religion in the public-school system and of theology professors in universities. Thus, from an economic point of view of least, the differentiation of the state and religious institutions has not yet taken place.

To apply the sub-theory of progressive decline of religious beliefs and practices concomitant with a progress of modernization, we need to pay attention to three distinct time periods: pre-communist, communist, and post-communist. The most acute decline of religious beliefs and practices occurred, as expected, under communism. Some attempts to introduce atheism in the form of freethought existed in pre-communist Romania, but they made an insignificant dent in religious beliefs and practices.[52] After the collapse of the communist regime, a dramatic increase in religious beliefs and practices took place as Romania entered a period of considerable modernization and democratization, when the dominant Orthodox religion became very public.[53] This religious growth appears to

---

52 Lucian Turcescu, "Romania: Between Freethought, Atheism and Religion," in *Freethought and Atheism in Central and Eastern Europe: The Development of Secularity and Non-Religion*, eds. Tomáš Bubík, Atko Remmel, and David Václavík (Abingdon, UK: Routledge, 2020), 207–32.

53 It is not the goal of this article to demonstrate how post-communist Romania has modernized. Other authors have already demonstrated that: Florin Abraham, *Romania since the Second World War: A Political, Social and Economic History* (London: Bloomsbury Academic, 2016); Maria Bucur-Deckard and Mihaela Miroiu, *Birth of Democratic Citizenship: Women and Power in Modern Romania* (Bloomington, IN: Indiana University Press, 2018); Henry F. Carey, *Romania since 1989: Politics, Economics, and Society* (Lanham, MD: Lexington Books, 2004); Monica Ciobanu, "Romania since 1989: Old Dillemmas, Present Challenges, Future Uncertainties," in *Central and East European Politics: From Communism to Democracy*, 4th ed., eds. Sharon L. Wolchik and Jane Leftwich Curry (Lanham, MD: Rowman & Lit-

be a permanent feature that continues even three decades after the collapse of communism.[54] This leads us to the third sub-theory, namely that privatization of religion is a precondition of secular and democratic politics. As noted already, religion is very public, with not just ordinary believers participating in public processions and pilgrimages, studying religion in public schools, but politicians also using religion openly especially during electoral campaigns in order to get votes from the citizens.[55]

Romania does not really fit the theory of secularization: its post-communist modernization and democratization have been accompanied by a religious revival; there is no religious decline or privatization of religion. But perhaps the most important aspect is that in the case of the first sub-theory, there does not appear to be a full institutional differentiation between the state and the church, when this is looked at from an economic perspective. Because Casanova contrasts the USA with European nations when it comes to various aspects of secularization he describes, it is in order to use the same argument in reference to Romania. In this regard, Romania differs from the United States, where the "wall of separation" between church and state prevents the use of public funds for religious purposes. Romania presents us with a type of informally dominant church model, where a state chooses to acknowledge as important a church that represents the majority of the population and treats it informally in a privileged manner.[56]

Like other formerly communist countries, Romania has witnessed a growth of religions in reaction to the previous attempts at secularization and elimination of religion that took place under communism, as well as a booming market of religious goods. The phenomenon taking place in that country can thus legitimately be viewed as a form of de-secularization in the religious realm, while the country has modernized in numerous other social and political aspects, particularly because of joining the European Union in 2007.

---

tlefield, 2018), 373–403; Duncan Light and David Phinnemore (eds), *Post-Communist Romania: Coming to Terms with Transition* (London: Palgrave Macmillan, 2001); Lavinia Stan and Diane Vancea, *Post-Communist Romania at Twenty-Five: Linking Past, Present, and Future* (Lanham, MD: Lexington Books, 2015); Economist Intelligence Unit, "Country Report: Romania" (report generated on April 13, 2020) (London: Economist Intelligence Unit, 2020).

54 Lucian Turcescu, "Eastern Orthodox Constructions of 'the West' in the Post-Communist Political Discourse: The Cases of the Romanian and Russian Orthodox Churches," in *Orthodox Constructions of the West*, eds. George Demacopoulos and Aristotle Papanikolaou (New York: Fordham University Press, 2013), 211–28.
55 Stan and Turcescu, *Religion and Politics in Post-Communist Romania*.
56 Ibid.

Conclusion

Reports on the financial and economic activities of the ROC will remain estimative in the absence of public access to the data submitted annually by the church to the Ministry of Finance. Public access might not even adequately address the issue, since the church's accounting practices lack transparency and consistency. The church will continue to hide its assets under the cloak of secrecy as long as it remains a national symbol for the citizens and a powerful electoral ally (or potential enemy) of the political elite. That is because the informal established church model that post-communist Romania has followed since 1989 places the church above other religious denominations and often above the state institutions mandated to verify its assets. This article has presented a summary of the church's financial and economic activities that are currently known to the public and can be reasonably documented. The reality might be more nuanced. The secularization test showed the secularization that took place in Romania under communism was almost completely reversed, and one can legitimately speak of de-secularization.

Shaping, Questioning, Contradicting "Bad Communism:" Aspects of Generational Memory in Romania after 1989

Valeska Bopp-Filimonov

Abstract: *Families in Romania, I was told when presenting my research topic in front of Romanian audiences in 2005, would not openly discuss the socialist past, neither within the family nor with a foreign researcher. My research—based on interviews with Romanian families—confirmed that different age groups remembered communism not only differently (which is to be expected due to variation in cohort and life experience), but also separately, and rarely shared their memories. Instead, what all interview accounts had in common was the extensive examination of the overall negative public discourse on "bad communism." This paper presents the respondents' particular strategies of examination, expanding our understanding of how the historical consciousness of a society in transition can be analyzed and understood. Of particular interest is how respondents reflected upon the socialist past, which came to an end in 1989.*

Introduction

This paper is based on comprehensive research on the parallel—and at the same time intertwined—"identity work" of individuals and society after the upheaval in the Romanian political system in 1989.[1] Romania presented itself as a particularly interesting case study compared to other socialist states, as its citizens were abruptly catapulted into the post-so-

---

1 Ulrike Jureit, "Identitätsarbeit. Ein Kommentar zu biographischen Erinnerungen in (post)sozialistischen Gesellschaften," in *Erinnerungen nach der Wende. Oral History und (post)sozialistische Gesellschaften*, eds. Julia Obertreis and Anke Stephan (Essen: Klartext, 2009), 85–90, 85. Valeska Bopp-Filimonov, *Erinnerungen an die ‚Nicht-Zeit'. Das sozialistische Rumänien im biographisch-zeitgeschichtlichen Gedächtnis (1989–2007)* (Wiesbaden: Harrassowitz Verlag, 2014). This paper refers most explicitly on chapter 4.2 "Wandel der Erinnerung. Aspekte des Generationengedächtnisses in Rumänien nach 1989", 272–92. The book is currently not available in English. Translation of the passages referenced in this article were provided by the author. I would like to thank the anonymous reviewers for important and useful remarks and Al Kupetz and Marcy Brink-Danan for proofreading the manuscript at different stages.

cialist era. Until December 1989, news about world political changes filtered into people's conversations only via foreign radio stations and, later, via rumors. Intimidated by the omnipresent surveillance of the Romanian secret service and tired by a decade of extreme shortages, no relevant reformist circles had emerged and alternative political options were only privately expressed, if at all. The starting point of the Revolution was a local conflict in the western Romanian city of Timișoara that escalated into major protests critical of the regime. Only then did people in Bucharest take to the streets and, eventually, also in other cities in the country.

The Romanian revolution was violent. The army and other security forces fired on the people, and even after President Nicolae Ceaușescu fled Bucharest by helicopter on December 22 and the army sided with the demonstrators, unidentified snipers killed people by shooting from roof balustrades and house windows. Not even the "death of the dictator" on December 25, 1989 calmed the situation.[2] The mixture of hope and relief, panic and fear, disbelief and surprise with which people experienced those days shapes the memory of the Revolution, leaving the meaning of the event inconclusive for most Romanians.[3]

If one considers Romanian public discourse (between 1989–2006), "communism" became a singular catchword for describing the past. In the second post-1989 decade, articles on shortages and censorship were titled "Everyday Life under Communism", post-socialist politics was called "Politics after Communism", and reference works were labeled "Archives of Communism."[4] The connotation of the term could be extremely negative, as in the case of the claim for a "condemnation of communism;" in some cases, over time, the need to reanimate this period and to understand it retrospectively also sounded as if a feeling of loss was expressed, as in the title "In Search of Lost Communism."[5] Kevin Adamson, a British

---

2   Armin Heinen, "Der Tod des Diktators und die Gegenwart der Vergangenheit. Rumänien 1989–2002," *Zeitblicke*, 3, no. 1 (2004), http://www.zeitenblicke.de/2004/01/heinen/index.html, accessed October 10, 2020.
3   Dragoș Petrescu, "Blutige Revolution, paradoxe Folgen. Der Umsturz in Rumänien 1989 und sein Erbe," *Osteuropa*, 69, no. 6–8 (2019), 93–104.
4   Adrian Neculau (ed), *Viața cotidiană în comunism* (București: Polirom, 2004). Alina Mungiu-Pippidi, *Politică după comunism* (București: Humanitas, 2002). Dan Cătănuș (ed), *Intelectuali români în arhivele comunismului* (București: Nemira, 2006).
5   *De ce trebuie condamnat comunismul*, Anuarul Institutului de Investigare a Crimelor Comunismului în România, vol. 1 (Iași: Polirom, 2006); Paul Cernat, Ion Manolescu, Angelo Mitchievici and Ioan Stanomir, *În căutarea comunismului pierdut* (Pitești: Editura Paralela 45, 2001). Even though this kind of nostalgia does not aim at restoration but is a kind of "reflexive nostalgia", searching to come to

political scientist, illustrates that the term "communism" is—with reference to Lacan—an "empty signifier" which allows a variety of connotations depending on the speaker and addressee. He examined the changes of the terms "Socialism/Communism," "Revolution," and "Transition" for Romania from 1944 to 1992 in a discourse analysis and emphasizes the relevance of the associated key signifiers with which these terms were combined. This were in particular the notions "Nation" and "People," but also "Prosperity," "Democracy," "Freedom," and "Development."[6] Only after 1989, did an overall negative connotation became dominant by key signifiers such as "Terror", "Securitate", "Surveillance", "Abortion", "Hunger" etc.[7] However, the headlines (like the above mentioned) reflect "a global assessment," and the question is in what words and meanings would individuals take up biographical events and frame their lives in the socialist period. The intersection of individual narrative, family accounts, and public discourse is of particular interest here.[8]

Methodological Approach

For Romanians, the period 2005–2007, when this research took place, can be described from a generational point of view, as a period "in between" which the cultural scientist Jan Assmann termed "communicative memory."[9] He thus characterizes the memory activity of societies that negotiate a time that the bearers of memory have largely experienced themselves. The historical events of the time are not yet interwoven into a common thread, but are still in the process of being interpreted and classified by the members of the respective society. The "communicative memory" is therefore characterized "by a high degree of unspecialization, role reciprocity, thematic vagueness and disorganization," as Assmann puts it.[10] According to Pennebaker and Banasic "this interaction process is critical

---

terms with one's own memories. See for the conceptual part Svetlana Boym, *The Future of Nostalgia* (New York: Basic Books, 2001).
6   Kevin Adamson, *Socialism, Revolution, and Transition. The Ideological Construction of the Romanian Post-Communist Order* (PhD thesis, University of Essex, 2004), 22.
7   For a more detailed investigation from my part see Bopp-Filimonov, *Erinnerungen*, 54–97.
8   Daniela Georgeta Oancea, *Mythen und Vergangenheit. Rumänien nach der Wende* (PhD thesis, Ludwig-Maximilians-Universität München, 2005), 187, http://edoc.ub.uni-muenchen.de/4577/, accessed 21 October 2020.
9   Jan Assmann, *Das kulturelle Gedächtnis. Schrift, Erinnerung und politische Identität in frühen Hochkulturen*, 5th ed. (München: C.H.Beck, 2007).
10 Quoted after Harald Welzer, "Das soziale Gedächtnis," in *Das soziale Gedächtnis. Geschichte, Erinnerung, Tradierung*, ed. Harald Welzer (Hamburg: Hamburger Edition, HIS 2001), 9–21, 15.

to the organization and assimilation of the event in the form of a collective narrative."[11]

The family has a special meaning as a social unit within which memory is tested, compared and negotiated. Harald Welzer, who has studied the "learning" of memory from the perspective of developmental psychology, refers to "memory talk" in which small children learn to describe past events.[12] The family is equally important in terms of habits and ways of thinking, which, as Halbwachs put it in the 1920s, can be "imposed" on the offspring by means of language, but can also be consolidated in family behavioral rites.[13] Thus, this immediate memory framework in which we grow up leaves a distinctive impression. Since each family member deals with the socio-political conditions of his or her time in an individual way and communicates this conflict to the family, a reconsideration of the connection between these levels seems to be extremely important to understand exactly what shapes the memory narrative.[14] To take these dynamics into account, the present sample consists of 45 interviews conducted with members of 18 families, so that the narratives of two or three family members could be related to each other.

The basis of the interpretation is detailed life history interviews, characterized by open-ended questioning about the interviewee's life history. The respondents choose which periods they want to focus on and also the amount of details provided. In the analysis, special interest lay in the narrative strategies people used to address their lives and I used the interview method's ability to highlight these findings. Oral historians and sociologists conducting biographic interviews consider the fundamentally dialectical disposition of the biography—as a life story, but also as a remembered narrative.[15] They offer detailed techniques how to reveal narrative strategies and to cluster interview samples by (narrative) types

---

11   James W. Pennebaker and Becky L. Banasic, "On the Creation and Maintenance of Collective Memories. History as Social Psychology," in *Collective Memory of Political Events. Social Psychological Perspectives,* eds. Dario Paez and Bernard Rimé (Mahwah, New Jersey: LEA Publishers 1997), 3–19, 4.
12   Harald Welzer, *Das kommunikative Gedächtnis. Eine Theorie der Erinnerung* (München: C.H. Beck, 2002), 92.
13   Maurice Halbwachs, *Das Gedächtnis und seine sozialen Bedingungen* (Frankfurt/Main: Suhrkamp 1985), 203–42, 209.
14   Gabriele Vierzigmann and Simone Kreher, "'Zwischen den Generationen' – Familiendynamik und Familiendiskurse in biographischen Erzählungen," *Berliner Journal für Soziologie,* no. 1 (1998): 23–37, 32.
15   Armin Nassehi, "Die Form der Biographie," *BIOS,* 7, no. 1 (1994): 46–63, 47–9: Gabriele Rosenthal, *Erlebte und erzählte Lebensgeschichte. Gestalt und Struktur biographischer Selbstbeschreibungen* (Frankfurt, New York: Campus, 1995).

of social demands, biographical crises or historical traumas.[16] And besides, there are works that thoroughly analyze generational coherences and also interdependencies of collective memory and memory practice.[17]

Informants were selected by the "snowball sample" method, i.e., the number of interviewees grew due to the fact that a person who took part proposed another acquaintance as a contact. This simplified the process and, more importantly, assured the necessary confidence for the approach and willingness of the participants to talk about their personal lives. The sample includes a wide range of professions and social backgrounds of the interviewees in order to be able to analyze as many possibilities as possible for referring to the post-1989 discourse critical of communism. The professional spectrum includes a publicist, politician, historian, physician, civil engineer, teacher, art critic, priest, architect, ministry staff, self-employed tourist manager, translator, doctors, housewife, salesman, saleswomen and secretary. Other variables such as gender, ethnicity, religion did not systematically guide the compilation of the overall sample, but were considered in the interpretation of each specific case.

The following analysis is organized according to three age cohorts or "generations". When using the term "generation," my understanding of this notion is pragmatic and interactive. In this, I follow scholars who emphasize the fact that generational affiliation is not only the result of experiencing the same historical occurrences, but reflects social negotiations

---

16   See, for instance, Lutz Niethammer, "Fragen – Antworten – Fragen. Methodische Erfahrungen und Erwägungen zur Oral History," in *"Wir kriegen jetzt andere Zeiten". Auf der Suche nach der Erfahrung des Volkes in nachfaschistischen Ländern*, eds. Lutz Niethammer and Alexander von Plato (Berlin, Bonn: Campus 1985), 392–445. Ulrike Jureit, *Konstruktion und Sinn. Methodische Überlegungen zu biographischen Sinnkonstruktionen*, Oldenburger Universitätsreden no. 103 (Oldenburg: BIS-Verlag, 1998); Rosenthal, *Erlebte und erzählte Lebensgeschichte*. Fritz Schütze, *Die Technik des narrativen Interviews in Interaktionsfeldstudien – dargestellt an einem Projekt zur Erforschung von kommunalen Machtstrukturen* (Bielefeld: Universität Bielefeld, Fakultät für Soziologie, 1977). Gabriele Lucius-Hoene und Arnulf Deppermann, *Rekonstruktion narrativer Identität. Ein Arbeitsbuch zur Analyse narrativer Interviews*, 2nd ed. (Wiesbaden: VS Verlag für Sozialwissenschaften, 2004).
17   See, for instance, the works of the German sociologist Gabriele Rosenthal, "Zur Interdependenz von kollektivem Gedächtnis und Erinnerungspraxis. Kultursoziologie aus biographietheoretischer Perspektive," in *Kultursoziologie. Paradigmen – Methoden – Fragestellungen*, ed. Monika Wohlrab-Sahr, 151–76 (Wiesbaden: VS Verlag für Sozialwissenschaften, 2010); Idem, "Social Transformation in the Context of Familial Experience. Biographical Consequences of a Denied Past in the Soviet Union," in *Biographies and the Division of Europe. Experience, Action, and Change on the 'Eastern Side'*, eds. Roswitha Breckner, Devorah Kalekin-Fishman and Ingrid Miethe, (Opladen: Leske + Budrich 2000), 115–38; Idem (ed.), *Der Holocaust im Leben von drei Generationen. Familien von Überlebenden der Shoah und von Nazi-Tätern* (Gießen: Psychosozial-Verlag, 1997).

and even concrete dialogues between individuals of different ages and, thus, a result of inter-generational attributions.[18] When Astrid (*1984), 22 years old at the time of the interview and one of my interviewees, tells her 5-year old brother Harald (*1993) in a very categorical tone, "But you, you don't know anything about communism," she distinguishes a (generational) boundary that can be understood in exactly this sense.[19] In the early 1990s, their parents had the impression that Romania was developing in a positive sense and decided to have little Harald. In the interview, they called him a "child of optimism", and indeed he experienced very different living conditions and social realities than his older brother and sister did, who were born in the 1980s. Nevertheless, it is interesting that Astrid claimed her early childhood to be crucial for her life experience and knowledge on that period.

This approach, which captures also family relations, shows how important it is to consider age and experience—and thus external historical reference points—and also demonstrates the opportunities for a nuanced picture, which results from allowing the subjects to have their say individually and from recognizing their agency. Investigations on public discourse and memory culture on the one hand and individual memory work on the other hand mostly coexist and are only rarely combined. If so, I agree with Alon Confino, that these histories "should be integrated without imposing congruency."[20] The following explanations show how different age groups perceived and shaped dominant public discourse in the early post-communist years and integrates, when possible, also findings on inner-familial dynamics.

Shaping and confirming the narrative of "bad communism"

It is the oldest peer group that most consistently affirmed that life under communist rule was not worth mentioning and, ultimately, a catastrophe for their family's life, interrupting all aspirations and undermining all

---

18 Karl Mannheim, "Das Problem der Generationen," *Kölner Vierteljahreshefte für Soziologie*, 7, no. 3 (1928): 157–85, 309–30, 313. Gabriele Rosenthal, "Zur interaktionellen Konstitution von Generationen. Generationenabfolgen in Familien von 1890–1970 in Deutschland", in *Generationen-Beziehungen, Austausch und Tradierung*, eds. Jürgen Mansel, Gabriele Rosenthal and Angelika Tölke (Opladen: Westdeutscher Verlag, 1997), 57–63.
19 Bopp-Filimonov, *Erinnerungen*, 291–292.
20 Alon Confino, "Telling About Germany: Narratives of Memory and Culture (Review Article)", *The Journal of Modern History*, 76, June (2004): 389–416, 411.

chances for a professional career and a prosperous life. The sample was small and consisted of seven interviewees born between 1919 and 1933 who hailed from urban environments and mainly academic or even aristocratic families. This explains why they remembered their childhood positively and painted the picture of a prosperous Romanian state in the interwar years. Statements like "Romania was a rich country" or a "beautiful country" entered into memories of generous living spaces and indicators of material prosperity, as well as family reunions and urban festivities. Throughout these memories, the monarchy appeared in a positive light; the then-young women reported how they were excited to see the nearly same-aged prince Mihai; the men mentioned proudly when their fathers or uncles were part of (or in contact with) the governing elite. Simply put, my interviewees in this cohort lived a childhood intended to prepare them to enter into exactly these same circles and, one day, become an elite member of Romanian society.

The connecting characteristic of the narratives was that these respondents talked mostly about their formative years in interwar Romania, while scarcely referencing their lives under socialism.[21] When considering the general findings of memory studies, there seems to be a tendency that older people look back nostalgically on the period of their childhood, not necessarily because life was better, but because to be young and cared for retrospectively seemed "better."[22] In this case, however, the positive point of reference of childhoods in the 1920s and 1930s fitted the officially accepted discourse in Romania at the beginning of the 1990s that idealized the interwar years as the golden age of the past. This way, their personal accounts resembled early public discourse on the interwar years, explained by Butoi, a Romanian sociologist, as follows:

> Immediately after 1989, the search for a point of reference that would help both to understand communism and to define the desired goal of a social re-foundation began, and this period appeared in the morning sky of collective consciousness of the highest economic and democratic development and cultural excellence. The myth was simple: Romania was successful and palpable on the ascending path, synchronizing itself with the West, a path that was suddenly and brutally interrupted by the entry into the Soviet sphere of rule and the installation of communism.[23]

---

21 I ignored my memos of these interviews for quite some time and it took me a second attempt to reconsider and identify which conclusions could be drawn from the glaring omission of 40 years of their life stories.
22 Andrea Fasching, "Die Glorifizierung der Kindheit in der Erinnerung älterer Menschen," in *Psychiatrie der Lebensabschnitte*, eds. H.G. Zapotoczky, P.K. Fischhof (Wien, New York: Springer-Verlag, 2002), 105–12.
23 Ionuț Butoi, "Epocalismul interbelic sau despre un mit bipolar," in *De ce este România astfel? Avatarurile excepționalismului românesc*, ed. Vintilă Mihăilescu (Iași: Polirom, 2017), 199–210, 202.

The respondents of the present sample introduced the suspension of their lives in nearly the same words: "when the Russians came ..." or "when the communists came ..." and remembered different episodes from this transition period in which Russian soldiers stole watches, relatives were imprisoned, or when parents or acquaintances lost their jobs. The interwar years retrospectively sounded like a lost paradise, whereas communism was "the beginning of the end."[24] They hardly reported on concrete changes in everyday life and preferred to talk about other people's suffering instead of their own experience.

While the men whom I interviewed hardly ever reported on any personal, subjective, or emotional moments from their lives in the socialist country, the three women were more willing to provide that information. Zoe's (*1922) biographic account stumbles from one misfortune to the next: her first husband left her as young mother for another woman, she suffered financial crises, had to go through a difficult operation with unexpected pain in the aftermath that made her consider suicide. Her son left Romania 1979 for a career as musician in Venezuela; her second marriage—with a former "public enemy" who had been imprisoned for 10 years—was not very happy. Eleonora (*1919) emphasizes suffering, for example, of her husband, who had (also) been imprisoned for a long time and then was a broken man, but legitimized also their adaptation to the socialist system—precisely as the result of this experience. Happiness and unhappiness are balanced in her memory narrative. Only Cosmina (*1919) declared her life as unrestrictedly happy. Despite the death of her first husband in the war and her second husband's detention under communist rule, she emphasized that she has lived completely comfortably and was always surrounded by affection. She talked about fashion and beauty and stressed that throughout her life, she had attached importance to stylish, high-quality clothing for herself and her children. She said that she never experienced any kind of shortage. During the interview she repeated a few times the sentence she had told me already when we arranged the date for our interview: "I emphasize once again: I had a happy life, from my first day until today." From the interpretation it was clear that she had decided not to engage in a narrative of her life as a "life under communism" for our conversation, but wanted to emphasize that this could not harm her as a person loved by her fellow man. It was her daughter who talked about the hardships her parents went through in the early

---

24 Adriana Georgescu, *La început a fost sfârșitul* (București: Humanitas, 2004). The book was originally published in French under the title "Au commencement était la fin" (Paris: Hachette, 1951), and appeared in Romanian for the first time in 1992.

years of communist Romania. Her father was no longer allowed to work in his office, which robbed the family of its livelihood. A friend helped him by arranging an income opportunity in the town of Miercurea Ciuc, 300 km away, where the family moved for a few years when the children were small. Eventually, they could return to Bucharest, but even when he resumed his work as a lawyer, one night the secret service suddenly appeared at the door to take him away. After another month he was released and life gradually returned to normal. According to his family, he was able to pursue his profession again very successfully. Again, unspoken compromises with the new regime are an invisible part of the story, as there must have been a price for the regained success.

In contrast to the women—Zoe, for example, said that she did not dare to talk about politics—the male respondents felt not only empowered, but called upon to evaluate and interpret politics and history. In their families, as could be seen by talking to their younger descendants, they were regarded as authorities and sources that are also consulted for the historical picture (much less about their own experiences). They emphasized the time "before the communists" as formative for their personality, in which important intellectuals and politicians had a formative effect on them. They grew into this world of (male) adults in order to one day take their places and also find fulfilment in their professions and participate in society. Not with tears, but with a calm, sometimes instructive style, they met the foreign female and also a much younger interviewer and explained Romania's decline under socialism.

Tudor (*1927) radiated calmness and friendliness while telling his life story. Later, I found sentences from our conversation in interviews he gave to Romanian newspaper journalists. This indicates that his life story was precisely set out. He hints at his experience of persecution in the early communist period, which seems to justify his authority in condemning the whole period. Neither the journalists nor I explicitly asked about (necessary) compromises in the course of his life. After all, Tudor successfully obtained a permanent position in academia, was able to complete his doctorate, and was honored with a prize for his PhD thesis by the Romanian Academy of Science. After the December 1989 revolution, he experienced a professional "upgrade" and immediately became the director of the scientific institution he had worked for as an employee.

In contrast to the impression gained from our personal encounter, in his political opinion articles he argues with relentless rigor against Romania's post-communist politicians with ties to the former pre-1989 political system. He sharply and repeatedly condemned communism in the newly established intellectual press, which was highly receptive to his statements and explanations about the history of Romania. It seemed that his credibility was enhanced by the serious terror his family members had experienced, and most notably the fact that he himself spent a few months in a prison camp at the Danube-Black Sea Canal where he was part of the forced workers recruited from political prisoners. It seemed that intellectuals like him had, with their pre-socialist socialization and the painful experience of becoming excluded from all relevant capitals (economic, social, political) a point of view that demanded a hearing after the "failure" of the system in 1989.

Thus, with his engagement in the media, he shaped the way the communist past was publicly remembered. It is this thread of discourse that Cristina and Dragoș Petrescu termed metaphorically the "Pitești syndrome," referring to communism "as a period of sheer terror and widespread repression."[25] On a personal level, the articles seemed to be the outlet he used to vent his anger over past injustices and I assume that this is the reason that he is able to be at peace with himself and very balanced in the personal encounter.

The other respondents with a similar social background, like the geophysicist Miron (*1925), and also the elderly Bucharest women born during interwar Romania, were the readers of Tudor's articles and altogether shared his perspective. But they come to partly different conclusions regarding the present. As they were not media or political elites and thus did not actively shape the post-1989-society, they were more pessimistic about Romania's future. They embraced a discourse based on the notion of a "loss." They felt they were a lost or victimized generation, leaning towards nationalistic points of view and orthodox Christianity. In contrast, intellectuals and politicians like Tudor and his nephew Dan who became actively engaged in the public sphere, gained public attention, and hence, satisfaction. They reached the places in society their parents once hoped that their sons would.

Questioning the narrative of "bad communism"

The second peer group sample was born between 1937 and 1966; most of the respondents grew up in the 1950s. For them, the socialist state was the only "way to be." In case they had academic or even aristocratic family

---

25 The term is a reference to (on its own, Pitești refers to the city) the "Pitești Experiment", a re-education project that was carried out in Pitești prison. Dragoș and Cristina Petrescu, "The Pitești syndrome—A Romanian Vergangenheitsbewältigung?," in *Postdiktatorische Geschichtskulturen im Süden und Osten Europas. Bestandsaufnahme und Forschungsperspektiven*, ed. Stefan Troebst (Göttingen: Wallstein Verlag, 2010), 502–618, 504.

backgrounds, their childhood memories begin with the harsh atmosphere of explicitly politicized everyday life shaped by the new communist ideology. In their youth, however, they grew up with the few liberal years of socialist Romania through the first years of Ceaușescu's reign and, congruent with their age as young adults, their aspirations grew to realize themselves and make the best out of their lives in a socialist country. Memories about the restrictions of the 1950s seem to have faded in that time period.[26] Only after having finished school, when they wanted to pursue their studies or choose a profession, apply for a fellowship or travel abroad, these wishes were denied, or they had to change their fields of study, and were thus "reminded" of their family's past.

The most important result is that most of the connections between their "social background" and individual life events essentially became clear to them after 1989, which in turn means that their parents did not always make them sufficiently transparent. Despite being generally aware of the fact that her family did not support the socialist system, Aurela's (*1955) world collapsed when she didn't get the university place she had dreamed of despite her excellent grades. She began to question herself instead of contextualizing her "failure" in the extant socio-political situation. She vividly remembered her family being terrorized by the Securitate in her childhood when the secret service staff searched her parents' house in the countryside for her uncle. He had been an anti-communist partisan from 1948–49, afterwards managed to live undiscovered in the woods, and then later worked on different construction sites under a false name. Only in 1964, when he read in the newspaper that political prisoners were amnestied, he decided to turn himself in to the authorities. Two years of imprisonment followed, until he was finally released. He subsequently recorded all the details in a "journal" that he wrote in the 1990s.[27] Aurela admitted that only when she read the whole story did the connections become clear to her. Apparently, her parents had concealed many connections in order to not endanger her or her uncle unnecessarily.

In retrospect, some of the interviewees criticized this protective silence not only about family histories but about the regime in general. Cristina (*1954), a doctor from Bucharest, tearfully remembered how shocked she was after 1989 by the formerly undisclosed information

---

26 Catherine Durandin describes how descendants from intellectual families adapted very well in *Istoria românilor* (Iași: Institutul European, 1998), 303; 306–7.
27 The family gave it to me for research purposes.

about the socialist country in which she lived. Addressing the armed resistance to the communist system in the 1950s, which became public after 1989, she accused her parents of not having told her about it: "I didn't know anything about that. But perhaps I would have had more courage if I had had such information, to think in different ways, to question the system more, to do something about it!" Dan (*1940), Tudor's nephew, reported that he was constantly aware of his family's aristocratic background: "Already in the 1950s, as a small child, I was interested in politics, because I saw what consequences this, this catastrophe brought, not only in the country, but also in my family." But even he emphasizes how late he learned of the extreme conditions of imprisonment that his closest relatives suffered and that he found out about the details of prison and release conditions only from the post-communist press and TV.[28]

Dan became an active member of the refounded Christian Democratic National Peasants' Party, which had existed in the interwar period and, like his uncle Tudor, Dan also became a publicist in the so-called anti-Communist press. In both the press and parliamentary speeches, he argued desperately against communism and repeatedly spoke out in favor of condemning officially the former political system. But unlike his uncle, he received no special recognition for this and much less respect (was instead teased in parliament).[29] Clearly, his generation did not have the same credibility as his uncle's when it comes to an assessment of the socialist past. He had, after all, not suffered physically, had acclaimed Ceausescu's condemnation of the Warsaw Pact invasion of Czechoslovakia in 1968, became thereupon even a member of the Communist Party. Even if he, like others, maintained an inherited mistrust in the socialist system, he lived a life (too) well-adapted to the society of his time.[30]

---

[28] See for instance the TV documentary "Memorialul Durerii" (The Memory of Pain) by Lucia Hossu Longin that was mentioned more than once by my interviewees. Delia Popescu presented a thorough analysis, "Victim talk and the purpose of memory: revisiting rhetoric in The Memorial of Pain", at the 2018 SRS conference "#Romania100—Looking Forward through the Past", 27 June 2018.

[29] Dan was a member of the Romanian Parliament from 1996–2000. In the interview he emphasized multiple times that he had "absolutely no success". For a detailed evaluation of his interventions in Parliament, see Bopp-Filimonov, *Erinnerungen*, 132–9.

[30] Cristina and Dragoș Petrescu have therefore initiated the term "post-communist anti-communists," "Mastering vs. Coming to Terms with the Past. A Critical Analysis of Post-Communist Romanian Historiography," in *Narratives Unbound. Historical Studies in Post-Communist Eastern Europe*, ed. Sorin Antohi (Budapest: CEU Press, 2007), 311–408.

For Aurela, it was also complicated. In the interview she discreetly criticized her uncle, the former partisan. Her family, which was expropriated under the communist regime, "had to bear an additional burden because of him." Her parents were no longer able to find jobs that corresponded to their abilities and interests, were threatened by the Securitate, and "finally, I don't know to what extent or whether—well, maybe it was better that way, but this matter has reached me, too" (referring to not obtaining the study place she had applied for). The public information about the partisans that became public in the 1990s triggered a process of reflection and understanding, but she finds it difficult to agree unconditionally with the public reading of the partisans as "heroes."[31] However, the family discourse is loyal towards her uncle and "the public," which "discovered" the partisans as an anti-communist movement after 1989 and turned them into patriots. This does not exactly make it opportune to put her own, comparatively lesser suffering in the foreground. And beyond that, there is another difficult topic that resonates with this uncle's past: He was inspired by the doctrine of the Legionary's movement, whose ideology divides contemporary public opinion. Historians who research fascist movements also clearly refer to the Romanian legionnaires' movement as such, while their self-portrayal since 1989 is as a patriotic federation, which served the nation in the 1930s–1940s and continues to do so.[32] By saying, "well, at that moment, I don't know what information he had, he was just a kid, but he fled into the mountains and joined one of these groups of resistance in the Făgărașer mountains," Aurela avoided making her own statement.

The whole interview sample gives evidence of the complex dialogue between what the respondents' families experienced and did (not) transmit, and what the interviewees found out from publicly available information after the regime change. Furthermore, the interviewees wanted to position themselves "correctly" in the present, but did not yet know ex-

---

31　See, for instance, Karl Heinz Brenndörfer, *Banditen, Spione oder Helden? Bewaffneter antikommunistischer Widerstand in Rumänien 1948–1962* (Stuttgart: K. H. Brenndörfer, 2005) or Vasile Motrescu and Mircea Dobre (eds.), *Jurnale din rezistența anticomunistă* (București: Nemira, 2006).

32　Armin Heinen, *Die Legion "Erzengel Michael" in Rumänien – Soziale Bewegung und politische Organisation: Ein Beitrag zum Problem des internationalen Faschismus* (München: Oldenbourg Wissenschaftsverlag, 1986). Oliver Jens Schmitt, *Căpitan Codreanu, Aufstieg und Fall des rumänischen Faschistenführers* (Wien: Zsolnay, 2016). Cecilie Endresen, *The Right-Winged Archangels of Romania: A Study of the Mystico-Fascist Legionary Movement after Communism* (M.A. thesis in History of Religion, University of Oslo, Institute for Cultural Studies, 2000).

actly how. Only a select few of the respondents with academic backgrounds shared their parents' radical denial of the communist system. Almost every one mentioned a "good communist" among his acquaintances who helped him out when he was in trouble. Some interviewees referenced this ambivalence as they ask themselves if they could have known more, if they should have lived differently. The oral accounts are sometimes confusingly disarranged, with an emphasis on the positive aspects and containing remarks that life was even better than now, followed by an apologetic explanation. For example, Andrea: (*1951): "don't get me wrong, I did not love communism. No. I am aware of the fact that it was a horrible system [...] and I often ask myself how my life would have been in a democratic country …"[33] Her life story is full of inner conflict. Adjectives in each paragraph alternated from "so nice" to "cruel" or "painful" or from "beautiful" to "horrendous."[34] But she, like most of the others, did not dare to question their parents' ways of life or ask for more details or explanations; likewise, their parents did not discuss these topics with them in detail. The purported collective anti-communist experience was an overwhelming theme present in the press and the book market after 1989, but among the sample's interviewees this did not lead to more intra-familial conversation on the topic of communism.[35]

Respondents whose parents were part of the working class or peasants were generally cautious when judging the communist system. They felt a sense of confirmation when they were granted distinctions at school or at work for good performance and they emphasized the difficulties for their non-academic parent before the communist rule. They also mentioned the opportunities that the communist system opened to them such as University studies and an academic career. Conversely, they did not know how to properly address these advantages as they were (also) aware now that these came at the expense of victims in other social strata. Public discourse condemning communism made it difficult for all interviewees to place any positive aspects under communism into their life accounts.

---

33 Bopp-Filimonov, *Erinnerungen*, 283–4.
34 See the impressive (nearly 850 words) comprehensive interview passage of Andrea, a foreign language teacher (*1951), illustrating this kind of narrative, in Bopp-Filimonov, *Erinnerungen*, 283–5.
35 Petrescu and Petrescu, *Pitești syndrome*.

Contradicting the narrative of "bad communism"

Interviewees from the youngest peer group were born between 1969 and 1989. The older they were, the more sophisticated and ambivalent their judgment of their experiences during communist times was. The younger the interviewees were, the more unbiased and untroubled they were. In the interview with Dan's son, Dominic (*1969), fragments of memory from the communist era had obviously made a strong impression, but were related neither in chronological order, nor following a fixed narrative scheme. This indicates that it was not yet possible for him to tell a coherent story. There is an almost continuous and intensive preoccupation with and examination of the (former) aristocratic family's attitudes. On the one hand, Dominic experienced his family as a strict educational authority, and on the other as a protective community space and living place where he felt comfortable and at home. Yet, the price of belonging was the recognition of the family's view of history, which Dominic uncritically adopted as a small child:

> The influence came only from my father, that is, completely. What they taught at school about communism ... I thought, I hated the Russians ... so much that I didn't even want to read Russian literature until I found Dostoevsky ... But I hated the Russians, what they did to us ...

In school, the adjectives "good" and "bad" were assigned differently for historical actors than in the transmission of history within the family—and he remembers vividly how his mother slapped him twice after he stubbornly repeated a few times the sentence, probably from a history class, "The boyars treated the farmers very badly." In the 1990s, Dominic studied political science and was active in the student league, organized conferences on the monarchy in Romania and, like his parents, wanted King Mihai, who had been forced into exile in 1947 and had become resident in Switzerland, return. The unexpected death of his father in 2006 made Dominic reconsider his career aspirations and engagement for political matters: "Now I'm very pessimistic. My father was always very optimistic; that is why he died. I haven't been like this since he died." His father, Dan, suffered a heart attack while attending a political meeting of the National Peasants' Party and had not been allowed to present a prepared statement on the necessary condemnation of the communist period. After that, Dominic said he could no longer look the people of this party in the eye and did not follow the advice to "continue doing what your father did." Instead, he set up his own small business and concentrated on his nuclear family. As much as Dominic was shocked by his father's death, and as negative as his attitude became regarding politics in Romania, it seemed to me as if, at the same time, he was relieved that the paternal authority, which also expected political commitment from him—in keeping with family tradition—did now fade.

Other, younger interview partners give themselves the appearance of being the decisive authority as administrators of family memory. Unsolicited, they indicated to me what their parents and grandparents would or would not want to talk about. They referred directly to (assumed) taboos in family memory. Some talked openly about the fact that they were born due to the lack of contraceptives and the dangers of illegal abortion. It did not prevent them from positively looking back at their childhoods. In their accounts, they explicitly state that it was their parents' responsibility to worry about food and other shortages. One common trope was the idea, in Mona's words (born 1978), that worrying about food and other consumer goods "stressed my mother, not me." This seemed to have been a strategy for defending an untroubled childhood, which was particularly common for those born in the 1980s.

Not specifically asked about supply shortages, most of them still clearly articulated that they were well-aware of the difficulties in obtaining certain goods. However, they asserted with complete conviction that they could always have exotic fruits, such as oranges, which were placed in a special room on the cupboard on the highest shelf. One young woman, Magdalena (*1979), even described how she gave away chocolate, oranges, and bananas to her schoolmates as she did not like them and had everything in abundance. Her parents were doctors, so they had better access to certain goods. The way she described her situation was all too demonstrative of an inclination to defend a normal childhood, obviously being tired of all the monotonous descriptions about the grey and bleak decade of Romania in the 1980s with which she was confronted from dominant public references.[36] The wish for a certain self-image is a powerful trigger to tell somehow skewed stories that do not necessarily meet with the prevalent reality.

---

36 See similar results on defending a 'normal childhood' in Cătălina Mihalache, "Talking Memories of the Socialist Age: School, Childhood, Regime", in *Remembering Communism. Private and Public Recollections of Lived Experience in Southeast Europe*, eds. Maria Todorova, Augusta Dimou, Stefan Troebst (Budapest, New York: CEU Press, 2014), 251–66, 258–61. Diana Georgescu explains thereby the popularity of blogs, online forums and Facebook groups "where memories of 'normal' life could finally be articulated." Diana Georgescu, *'Ceaușescu's Children:' The Making and Unmaking of Romania's last Socialist Generation (1965–2010)* (PhD dissertation, University of Illinois at Urbana-Champaign, 2015), 399. The perspective of

These young adults also vividly remembered the communist regime's school and youth organizations, the festivities that took place on the occasion of the national holiday on August 23, or at the beginning of the school year, and the propaganda events at which sometimes only preselected groups could participate. Ana's (*1977) dialogue with her father, which she attended, is an illustrative example of how the public negative discourse and a certain desired self-portrayal, led to a supposed "common" father-daughter evaluation of the story that was de facto completely different:

> *Ana:* I remember how I became a pioneer and how I, uh, and I had to recite a poem about the [communist] party in front of the current military academy there in *Cotroceni*, at *Militari*. Because the school was nearby, there was a ceremony. Well, we had [school] uniforms. I had been elected as class president, in the second grade, I did not yet know what responsibility uhm ... Actually no, no one had no responsibility at all. Children were so um ...
> *Cornel:* Because you were a model student.
> *Ana:* I also hated communism, listened to Europe liberă together with my parents, I remember that well (laughs).
> *Cornel:* [Laughs]

Both laughed, but Cornel seemed surprised; he had never mentioned hatred for Communism, but instead was about to explain that his daughter had very good grades. Ana instead was interested in distancing herself from the communist system and overheard her father's interjection. It seems to be a typical pattern for young people to remember what they think they heard or know, but what is not necessarily the essential point made by their parents.[37]

Instead, Aurela's daughter Simina (*1980) still remembered her tears when her mother forbade her to be one of the girls giving flowers to Nicolae Ceaușescu. She said, "Not even now do I understand her." On the other hand, for her, her granduncle who had been an anti-communist partisan, was a hero and an impressive adventurer. Since she found out about his life, she condemns her parents' comparatively modest critique of the socialist regime. She neither perceived the ambiguity of her mother nor noticed her own contradictory attitude. Similarly, Valentina (*1987) blamed her parents for having been careless when they took her, a six months old baby, to protests in the 1990s against the National Salvation

---

a psychologist adds Oltea Joja, "Den Kommunismus erinnern. Bilder und Vorstellungen in der Gegenwart", in *Zwischen Amnesie und Nostalgie: die Erinnerung an den Kommunismus in Südosteuropa,* eds. Ulf Brunnbauer and Stefan Troebst (Köln et.al.: Böhlau Verlag, 2007), 237–46.

37 Welzer, *Soziales Gedächtnis,* 17.

Front (FSN) and its leader, Ion Iliescu, in the 1990s. Yet, earlier in the interview she wondered why her parents did not rebel against the communist system.

Antonia from Timișoara (*1980) said that she sometimes wondered what might have become of her and all the children of her generation if the socialist system had continued to exist. She stated, thoughtfully, that her generation had probably come closest to what was called the "new (socialist) man," because she and her schoolmates had been so confident about everything they were told at school and believed what they were told.[38] As mentioned earlier with reference to the respondents born in interwar Romania, childhood is an important point of reference in peoples' biographies. While the oldest people interviewed were lucky to have spent their childhood in a period was widely remembered positively in the post-1989 Romanian society, the children born and raised in the 1980s have to "defend" the positive moments of their childhoods against a widely spread negative perception of the period.

The two youngest interviewees, Stefan and Raluca (both born in 1989), expressed the least interest in the communist period. Stefan shyly reports some of his family's experiences, but above all refers to his grandfather who, he said, was very much interested in history. Raluca's mother, a very talkative woman, had already told me that "the child" was only interested in the computer and not in books or the past. Raluca and Stefan only selectively refer to the presence of the past-and cite teachers who draw comparisons between the time before 1989 and the present, or people in the street who would rant about Ceaușescu, or inversely, consider the present more uncertain and less glorious. They cited snatched up statements without ever having questioned them.[39]

---

38 Bopp-Filimonov, *Erinnerungen*, 287.
39 Albena Hranova wrote an interesting article on her research results of "Remembering Communism" of Bulgarians, born in the late 1980s. In the period 2006–2008 (nearly the same time I conducted my interviews) she asked 159 students to write an ad hoc essay "telling a story from the socialist period." Afterwards she came across many misconceptions "about the general and conceptual terms ... but also about the everyday and political vocabulary of the period" and a memory she classified as "loan memory", i.e. stories the students heard from relatives or acquaintances. Albena Hranova, "'Loan Memory': Communism and the Youngest Generation," in *Remembering Communism*, 233–249. This fits with Welzer's assessment: "Communicative transmission of the past transports history en passant, unnoticed by the speakers, incidentally, unintentional". Welzer, *Soziales Gedächtnis*, 17.

Summary

This paper focused on the different ways in which various peer groups behaved during the communist era and argued about the powerful public narrative of "bad communism." The author's findings confirm that the intense memory activity with countless publications motivated by "a growing demand for the 'true' history" that emerged in the public in the 1990s did not find its mirror in more family discussions; rather, my respondents dealt mostly individually—rather than socially—with new information gathered after 1989.[40] At the same time, they all related—more or less explicitly—to the post-1989 public discourse that is characterized by the claim that "communism" was an externally imposed political system foreign to the Romanians and thus "a dark chapter of our past."[41]

Individuals who were *raised in interwar Romania* belong to the "shapers," "agents," and "certifiers" of this powerful thread of discourse; individuals *raised in the first decades of socialist Romania* presented themselves as "doubters" who were highly uncertain how to bring together positive memories of that era with their knowledge about communist atrocities. Individuals *raised in the last decades of socialist Romania* approached the topic either analytically, with clarity and (self-)confidently, or if they were younger, rejecting claims of any historical challenges, even given the existence of the (overwhelmingly present) shortages during the 1980s.[42]

---

40   Cristina Petrescu and Dragoș Petrescu, "Mastering vs. Coming to Terms with the Past: A Critical Analysis of Post-Communist Romanian Historiographie," in *Narratives Unbound. Historical Studies in Post-Communist Eastern Europe*, eds. Sorin Antohi, Baláczs Trencsényi and Péter Apor (Budapest, New York: CEU Press, 2007), 318.

41   For an overview of postcommunist politics and discourse see Cristina and Dragoș Petrescu, "The Canon of Remembering Romanian Communism: From Autobiographical Recollections to Collective Representations," in *Remembering Communism*, 43–70. Opening remarks of Romanian president Traian Băsescu at the Parliamentary Session on December 18, 2006, in which he, in his function "as Romanian head of state, [...] explicitly and categorically condemned the Romanian communist system", in Vladimir Tismăneanu, Dorin Dobrincu, Cristian Vasile (eds.), *Comisia Prezidențială pentru Analiza Dictaturii Comuniste din România. Raport final* (București: Humanitas, 2007), 11 and 15.

42   Codruța Alina Pohrib describes and analyzes two very popular Facebook groups addressing childhoods in the 1980s. She argues that this kind of (affirmative) activity employed in coping with the past is a "palliative for dominant accounts about the utter senselessness of the recent past". Alina Codruța Pohrib, "The Romanian 'Latchkey-Generation' writes back. Memory genres of post-communism on Facebook", *Memory Studies*, 12, no. 2 (2019): 164–183, 174, https://journals.sagepub.com/doi/pdf/10.1177/1750698017709869, accessed 7 October 2020. See also

The sample on which the study is based is not representative in a sociological sense. Opinion polls have repeatedly shown that about 60% of Romanians think that "communism was a good idea;" often the rural areas express above-average identification with this opinion.[43] Still, the in-depth interviews conducted for this study allow for some level of generalization and will hopefully stimulate further research and discussion on the topic. Meanwhile, a new generation has emerged since the overthrow of Romanian communist rule in December 1989. The increasing distance in time from the socialist past might make it easier to ask witnesses about that past, now that they had even more time to "put things into place." Besides, in recent years, at the many major rallies of the "anti-establishment protest cycle," demonstrators have repeatedly referred to the communist era and the revolution of 1989 on their posters critical of the government.[44] This shows that for many, the time has not yet been forgotten.

Cristina Petrescu, "Websites of Memory: In Search of the Forgotten Past", in *Remembering Communism*, 595–613.

43 See for instance Vladimir Tismăneanu, "Cum percep românii comunismul? Un nou sondaj IICCMER-CSOP," February 25, 2012, http://www.contributors.ro/politica-doctrine/cum-percep-romanii-comunismul-un-nou-sondaj-iiccmer-csop/, accessed 15 June 2018.

44 Ruxandra Gubernat & Henry Rammelt, "Romania's Protest Culture 30 Years after the Regime Change: Hegemonic Discourses and Western Ideals", in *Thirty Years After—Post Communism, Democracy and Illiberalism in Central and Eastern Europe*, ed. Daniela Popescu (London: Palgrave Macmillan, forthcoming).

Re-Envisioning Cubism in Romanian Avant-Garde Magazines

Amelia Miholca

Abstract: *Art historians and literary scholars have written little about the relationship between Cubism and the Romanian avant-garde. This paper seeks to remedy this oversight by analyzing images of cubist paintings and theoretical texts about Cubism, published by the Romanian avant-garde magazines Contimporanul and Integral, the platforms for the Romanian avant-garde and the magazines containing the most cubist art in the early to mid-1920s. The considerable amount of cubist artworks, via photographic reproductions, in Contimporanul and Integral point to a serious engagement with Cubism on behalf of Romanian avant-garde artists. Specifically, artists and magazine editors Marcel Iancu of Contimporanul and M.H. Maxy of Integral exalted Cubism's prominence in the formal development of avant-garde art while producing cubist still lifes and portraits, akin to the cubist paintings of Pablo Picasso and Georges Braque. Their unusual turn to Cubism at the stage of the movement when critics and artists began to see Cubism as out-of-date signifies not only the stylistic hybridity of the Romanian avant-gardists but also their willingness to traverse the space between avant-garde and modern art as they sought to conceptualize their integralist art.*

Introduction

The modernist avant-garde in Romania thrived in the 1920s through the publication of avant-garde magazines, which merged art and literature and belonged to a global network of avant-garde magazines that spanned multiple continents. Romanian writer Tristan Tzara and Romanian artist Marcel Iancu represented the Romanian avant-garde in the Dada movement in Zurich, 1916–1919. Afterwards, the two expanded Dada to Romania where it coalesced with the avant-garde Cubism and Constructivism in the paintings and prints that were reproduced in Romanian avant-garde magazines.[1] The magazine *Contimporanul* (*The Contemporary*), edited by Marcel Iancu and Ion Vinea, was the stronghold of the Romanian

---

1   The Romanian avant-garde magazines are *Contimporanul* (1922–1932); *75HP* (1924); *Punct* (1924–1925); *Integral* (1925–1928); *Puntea de Fildeș* (1925–1926); *Urmuz* (1928); and *Unu* (1928–1933).

avant-garde, publishing art by internationally renowned artists like Pablo Picasso and Georges Braque and by numerous Romanian artists like Marcel Iancu, M.H. Maxy, and Victor Brauner, whose careers would later flourish in Romania and abroad.[2] *Integral* (*Integral*) magazine, edited by a group of artists and writers in Bucharest and Paris, among them M.H. Maxy, followed in the footsteps of *Contimporanul* by publishing constructivist and cubist art, but it did so under its umbrella concept of Integralism.

In this paper, I argue that in the 1920s Romanian avant-garde artists, particularly the artists M.H. Maxy and Marcel Iancu, engaged with Cubism, as an avant-garde catalyst and a modern movement, to create integralist art that did not strictly adhere to one art style, neither avant-garde nor modern. A clear timeline of the impact of Cubism and successive avant-garde movements does not exist in Romanian avant-garde art because they all intersect. To determine the extent of the Romanian avant-garde artists' interaction with Cubism, I will primarily focus on the magazines *Contimporanul* and *Integral*. Of all the Romanian avant-garde magazines of the 1920s, these two published the majority of Romanian cubist art and thus were among Cubism's strongest proponents in Romania.

I use the term integralist art to denote an overarching style that arises from the synthesis of different stylistic elements, such as cubist, figurative, and constructivist elements. Iancu and Maxy's cubist art was a synthesis of styles which they termed Integralism, a notion associated with the *Integral* magazine that prevailed in the avant-gardists' art. Integralism acted as the foundation for Romanian avant-garde's artistic experimentation in the 1920s. It is "synthetic order, essential constructive order, classic, integral," in "rhythm with the times."[3] Reading the magazines, one may venture that Integralism is a Romanian variant of Constructivism, as some authors wrote, particularly in *Integral* issue no. 8, September 1925. In that issue, Mihail Cosma has a conversation with the famed Italian dramatist Luigi Pirandello, explaining to him that Integralism is "a scientific and objective synthesis of all aesthetic efforts attempted

---

2 Marcel Iancu, known outside Romania as Marcel Janco, was instrumental in establishing modern Israeli art after his emigration to Israel in 1941. Victor Brauner became a prominent artist of French Surrealism in Paris. M.H. Maxy stayed in Bucharest where he continued, despite discrimination due to the rise of antisemitism and fascism in Romania, to explore his modernist avant-garde practice through the precepts of Socialist Realism and later became the director of the National Museum of Art of Romania.

3 Ilarie Voronca, "Suprarealism si Integralism" ("Surrealism and Integralism"), *Integral*, no. 1, (March 1924): 5.

until the present ... on constructivist fundamentals."[4] In another Integral essay, Cosma writes that Cubism is "old art" as opposed to the "new art" of Integralism.[5] This new art tendency that the Romanian avant-gardists invented in and named after *Integral*, is meant to set Romanian avant-garde art apart from other avant-garde tendencies.[6] Ion Vinea also mentions integralist art in *Contimporanul*. It was both Cosma and Vinea's way of demonstrating their absorption of and mastery of these tendencies with an all-encompassing "ism." Integralism may have stemmed from Constructivism, as Voronca surmises, but the avant-gardists' constructivist art also overlaps with their cubist practice in their attempt to create integralist art.

The Modern and Avant-Garde Status of Cubism

An important question for this study is whether Romanian avant-garde artists and their magazines should or should not be thought of as avant-garde because of their adoption of cubist art. At the root of this question lies the debate on Cubism's position in the historical avant-garde. If Cubism is not an avant-garde movement, then the Romanian artists' identity as avant-garde needs to be reconsidered in light of their substantial engagement with Cubism. If Cubism, despite its superstar status in the canon of modern art, can be reevaluated with the concept of the avant-garde in mind, then the Romanian artists' cubist art is not so incompatible with the dadaist and cubist content in the avant-garde magazines.

Before we delve into how the Romanian avant-gardists used Cubism, it is important to briefly define Cubism and understand in which aspect of Cubism the Romanian avant-gardists were most interested. The definition of what Cubism is or what constitutes Cubism has changed over the past ninety years or so. In 1936, Alfred H. Barr Jr. divided Cubism into Analytic Cubism and Synthetic Cubism based on the artworks that Georges Braque and Pablo Picasso completed between 1908 and 1914. As Christopher Green describes it, the Analytic Cubism of Braque and Picasso dismantled the painted image "through a part-by-part analysis, involving the shifting of viewpoints." In Synthetic Cubism, the two artists built up images in their collages and *papier collés* "from schematic conceptual

---

4   Mihail Cosma, "De Vorba cu Luigi Pirandello," ("In Conversation with Luigi Pirandello"), *Integral* no. 8 (September 1925): 3.
5   Mihail Cosma, "De la futurism la integralism" "(From Futurism to Integralism"), *Integral*, no. 6–7 (October 1925): 9.
6   Ion Vinea, "Manifest Activist Către Tinerime" (Activist Manifesto for the Youth), *Contimporanul*, no. 46 (May 1924).

signs."[7] Green contends that the way in which Barr interpreted Cubism, and which art historians afterwards adopted, shifted when William Rubin argued for Cubism's "capacity to suggest depth while keeping a strong sense of the actual flatness of the picture surface" through the device of "passage" wherein parts of a painting's composition slide into each other.[8] Rubin's formalist approach to defining Cubism according to the primacy of perception over conception differs from not only Barr's approach but also to those of Guillaume Apollinaire, André Salmon, and the Salon Cubists.[9] They valued Cubism's conceptual, scientific knowledge in overcoming "the handicap of the eye" while depicting the fourth dimension through multiple spatial views.[10]

I posit that Romanian avant-garde artists were more concerned with the formal aspects of Cubism, its internal relationships between objects—the "autonomy and internal logic of the picture object" that for cubist art dealer Daniel-Henry Kahnweiler defined cubist art—and its flattening of the picture plane.[11] Consequently, I will not discuss the scientific interpretation nor, more importantly, the semiotic interpretation of Cubism that has been central to our most recent understanding of Cubism, particularly of cubist collages and *papier collés* that are missing from Romanian cubist art. Additionally, Cubism continued once Synthetic Cubism ended but discourse on art history has little to say on this long period of late Cubism that lingered during WWI and well into the 1920s. The editors of *Art Since 1900* assigned this period only a few pages, covering the classicism of Cubism, as evidenced in Picasso and Gris's structurally rigid paintings that they created in post WWI-France and its "rappel a l'ordre" (return to order) environment.[12] Green calls this postwar period a "late distilled form" of Cubism in which Picasso abstracted "from an already synthetic, if far more variegated, starting-point," and used "simple combinations of shapes which could act as signs for figures and objects."[13] Ultimately, as Green rightly points out, there is not an "essential Cubism" but different kinds of Cubism, as evidence by the Romanian version.[14]

---

7   Christopher Green, *Art in France* (New Haven: Yale University Press, 2000), 25.
8   Ibid., 24.
9   See Guillaume Apollinaire's 1913 book *The Cubist Painters: Aesthetic Meditation*; André Salmon's 1912 essay "Anecdotal History of Cubism"; Jean Metzinger and Albert Gleizes's 1912 essay "On Cubism."
10 Hal Foster, Rosalind Krauss, Yve-Alain Bois, and Benjamin H.D. Buchloh, (eds.), *Art Since 1900: 1900-1944*, Second Edition, Vol. 1 (Thames & Hudson: New York, 2011), 107.
11 Ibid., 109.
12 Ibid., 166-71.
13 Christopher Green, *Cubism and its Enemies: Modern Art Movements and Reaction in French Art, 1916-1928* (New Haven and London: Yale University Press, 1987), 16.
14 Green, *Art in France*, 25.

Within the context of Marcel Duchamp's painting period of 1911–1913, Thierry de Duve makes a case for Cubism's "monopoly of the avant-garde," led by Picasso and Braque in 1911.[15] De Duve links the avant-garde with the "need to innovate," to disregard the "current taste" of art institutions because "pictorial innovation is significant only if it finds itself rejected, at least a bit, by those institutions that dictate taste."[16] Cubism became an avant-garde movement because official art institutions rejected it. Meanwhile, the Salon embraced "the cubist avant-garde," composed of the salon Cubists Albert Gleizes, Jean Metzinger, and Henri Le Fauconnier who manifested the "contemporary history of art" at the Indépendants in opposition to Pablo Picasso, Georges Braque, Juan Gris, and Fernand Léger who exhibited exclusively at the Daniel-Henry Kahnweiler's gallery.[17] Hence, the Indépendants' rejection of Duchamp's *Nude Descending a Staircase no. 2* was also the "cubist establishment's" rejection of his painting.[18] We can surmise de Duve means by the cubists' manifestation of this history is that the cubists had a mighty hand in leading and dictating contemporary art at the Indépendants—already demonstrating the movement's indispensability, only a few years after its inception.

The institutionalization of Cubism was definitive with the 1936 exhibition "Cubism and Abstract Art" at the Museum of Modern art in New York. The exhibition's curator Alfred H. Barr Jr. presented Cubism's history in a chart: from its Analytic to its Synthetic periods, and previous art movements and artists, like Cézanne's Neo-Impressionism, to the art movements that sprang from Cubism, like Futurism and Constructivism. The chart solidified the Museum of Modern Art's vital role as the creator and carrier of the history of modern art. It also solidified Cubism as the foremost modern art movement in history.

In de Duve's interpretation of the concept of the avant-garde, Cubism's pictorial innovation in painting granted it its distinction as avant-garde, regardless of Cubism's institutionalization. Yet, this distinction only applies to Cubism's 1911–1913 period, or so de Duve implies, for it is his single focus. Going along, then, with de Duve's interpretation of Cubism, it is worth arguing that Cubism was an avant-garde in the beginning, due to its shocking, radical overturn of perspective and optical illusion,

---

15 Thierry de Duve, *Pictorial Nominalism: On Marcel Duchamp's Passage from Painting to the Readymade*, translated by Dana Polan (Minneapolis and Oxford: University of Minnesota Press, 2005), 21.
16 Ibid., 26.
17 Ibid., 25.
18 Ibid.

and its dissection and interrogation of the picture as a faithful representation of known reality. Its reinvention of the picture created a ripple effect throughout the art world.

Although the aftermath of Cubism's formal radicalism affected Romanian art well into the 1920s, its avant-garde status plummeted once its analytic and synthetic Cubism periods ended. Picasso and Braque began their separate cubist practices while abstract art began its ascent. Patricia Leighten, in her assessment of Cubism's historiography, identifies the shift in Cubism's history from a movement tied to the specific setting of modernity and modern subjects to a strictly formalist movement. Picasso reconstructed Cubism's history post-World War I. Art historians and critics went along with his "reductive view—art as a merely formal game—that has further distorted an understanding of the historical and intellectual milieu in which prewar cubist art developed."[19] That said, the Dadaists attached political and philosophical connotations to Cubism, because of Cubism's renunciation of painting's bourgeois morality and its insistence of the banality of daily existence through its *papier collés*.[20] Leighten surmises that in the eyes of the Dadaists, Picasso was a "self-conscious revolutionary and antitraditionalist"—an appropriate description of an avant-gardist.[21]

Though one may assume that Barr bolstered Cubism as primarily formalist, Leighten makes the case that Barr thought beyond the formal in pondering whether Cubism's subject matter of the artists' café environment signified the "isolation of the artist."[22] However, he claims the opposite in the *Cubism and Abstract Art* exhibition catalogue, writing: "The Cubists seem to have had little conscious effort in subject matter."[23] Susan Noyes Platt, in her account of the exhibition, reveals that Barr had a predilection for post-World War I realism. But he chose to eliminate it from his chart in order to heighten Cubism's influence on abstract art.[24] It is likely that in the exhibition Barr overlooked Cubism's subject matter and cultural context and pushed it towards a formalist history to show a reasonably direct line from its "near abstraction," wherein "natural forms" become abstract, to the "pure-abstraction" of Malevich, Mondrian, Gabo,

---

19 Patricia Leighten, "Revising Cubism," *Art Journal*, vol. 47, no. 4, (Winter 1988): 270.
20 Ibid., 271.
21 Ibid.
22 Ibid., 272.
23 Alfred H. Barr Jr, *Cubism and Abstract Art*, Exhibition Catalogue (New York: The Museum of Modern Art, 1936), 15.
24 Susan Noyes Platt, "Modernism, Formalism, and Politics: The "Cubism and Abstract Art" Exhibition of 1936 at the Museum of Modern art," *Art Journal*, vol. 47, no. 4, *Revising Cubism* (Winter 1988): 289.

and Kandinsky.²⁵ For Barr, Picasso's 1913 *Head of a Young Woman* epitomized the switch from Analytic to Synthetic Cubism, as it "moves from three dimensional, modeled, recognizable images to two-dimensional, flat, linear form, so abstract as to seem nearer geometry than representation."²⁶ The cubist subject retreats as form reaches its abstract conclusion. Although Barr admits that Cubism "consistently stopped short of complete abstraction," he insists that the flatness of form in cubist artworks, notably Picasso's, continued after 1914.²⁷

This flatness is discernible in Marcel Iancu and M.H. Maxy's cubist paintings, which gravitate towards postwar Synthetic Cubism, rather than the "near abstraction" of Picasso's *Head of a Young Woman*. As abstraction took hold of the avant-garde, Iancu and Maxy chose a different course, not the figurative representations of Surrealism but Cubism. Iancu's 1922 essay "Notes on Painting" from 1922 and Maxy's 1924 essay "Pictorial Timekeeping" anticipated Barr's history of Cubism, in which Cubism is the ancestor of abstract art. Yet, both artists eventually turned their backs on abstract art with their cubist paintings. Romanian art in the 1920s belies Barr's history. Not only in Romania, but also in other East-Central European countries, artists continued a cubist practice. For instance, Latvian artist Romans Suta, "the chief proponent of Latvian modernism," combined Cubism and Suprematism in his still lifes and portraits of the early 1920s.²⁸ In Czechoslovakia, artists such as Josef Čapek, Emil Filla, and Vincenc Beneš, working throughout the 1910s, produced a myriad of cubist woodcut and linocut prints with representational elements.²⁹ They produced "a broader and more individual conception of Cubism" after their initial infatuation with Braque and Picasso's Analytic Cubism. This conception leaned on the materials and techniques of printing and Czech art's history with Czech Symbolism.³⁰

None of the artists mentioned above worked with collage and *papier collés* and all retained traditional subject matter in their artworks. Perhaps these artists were attached to the medium of painting, but the cubist Czech prints negate this assumption. Additionally, though there are many more artists in East-Central Europe who worked in the cubist style, the

---

25   Barr, *Cubism and Abstract Art*, 12.
26   Ibid., 31.
27   Ibid., 92.
28   Vojtěch Lahoda, "Migration of Images: Private Collections of Modernism and Avant-Garde and the Search for Cubism in Eastern Europe," *Decentring the Avant-Garde*, ed. Per Bäckström (Amsterdam: Rodopi, 2014), 191.
29   For more information on each artist's prints, see Jana Wittlichová's "Czech Cubist Prints," *Print Quarterly*, vol. 5, no. 2 (June 1988): 127–47.
30   Ibid., 131.

Czech artists' prints exemplify a consistent experimentation with Cubism in a non-painting medium—that which is missing in Iancu and Maxy's cubist oeuvre. Iancu and Maxy worked in different mediums and fields, but when it came to Cubism they did not produce collages, *papier collés*, or prints. In the summer before World War I, Picasso and Braque ceased to make *papier collés* with their references to modern life's consumer culture. Rather than make *papier collés* with newspaper clippings of mass war casualties, they returned to the medium of painting, influenced by the history of nineteenth-century French painting.[31] Due to the difference in time, Iancu and Maxy's refusal surely does not signify any avoidance of a confrontation with the war. Iancu and his Dadaist friends already confronted it in their anarchist artistic acts. Maxy addressed the war indirectly in his paintings of post-war Romania and its dichotomy between industrial laborers and peasants.

Iancu and Maxy's refusal to experiment with and combine different mediums suggests a predilection for mastery of a specific medium. In his Zurich Dada days, Iancu went beyond painting and sculpture to create masks with low-brow materials like cardboard and twine, and abstract constructions with wood and plaster. In his role as the founder of the Studio of *Integral* magazine and as director of the Academia Artelor Decorative (Decorative Arts Academy), Maxy advocated for the integration of decorative arts into fine art. Be that as it may, Maxy and Iancu relied on the traditional medium of oil on canvas for their cubist paintings, which they reproduced in their magazines, with the exception of Iancu's cubist rendering on glass in *Contimporanul* issue no. 70, 1926.

According to Christopher Green, the Dadaists and Surrealists, through their practice with chance and automatism, opposed Cubism's modernist notion of the "autonomy of the artwork," its "pure painting," and the primacy of the artist. For them, cubist art was "too material," for it did not leave room for the imagination.[32] Cubism was still consequential from 1918 to 1925, but Dada and Surrealism posed a "serious threat" to Cubism's "avant-garde status and identity" from 1924 onwards.[33] Maxy and Iancu, though, viewed Cubism as a movement of "reform" and "resistance"—qualities that characterize the avant-garde—in the sense that they saw Cubism as means of reforming old ways of artmaking while up-

---

31 Christopher Green, "The Crystal in the Flame: Cubism and the 1914–18 War," in *Cubism and War: The Crystal in the Flame*, exhibition catalogue, ed. Christopher Green, Neil Cox, Giovanni Casini (Barcelona: Ediciones Poligrafa, 2016), 17.
32 Ibid., 273.
33 Ibid., 221.

holding a powerful resistance to detractors who disparaged any artmaking that was not within the prescribed guidelines of what viewers were commonly used to seeing in art, as in naturalist and impressionist portraits and landscapes by other Romanian artists. Cubist art was such a divergence from these traditional styles of art in Romania that for Romanian artists Cubism must have seem a provocateur to the established art order at that time. Maxy and Iancu must have viewed the late cubist period of the 1920s in the same way because they created their cubist works in this period.

What may be at play in this complicated debate over the avant-garde versus modernist qualities of cubism is the Romanian avant-gardists' use of the two concepts interchangeably. For example, *Punct* issue no. 16, March 1925, announced the merger of the magazine with *Contimporanul* in order to increase their "modern effort in Romania."[34] *75HP* magazine, the most radical of all the Romanian avant-garde magazines, is the only one to call itself "the unique avant-garde group of Romania."[35] It is tempting to draw a distinct delineation between those who were avant-garde, i.e., the *75HP* group, and those who were more modernist in their artistic approach, i.e., the rest of the magazines and their editors and contributors. Nevertheless, this distinction is futile because Maxy contributed his art to *75HP* while Iancu contributed to *Punct* and the rest of the magazines. Iancu may be less avant-garde than Maxy because he did not publish in *75HP*, but his constructivist art in the other magazines is on par with Maxy's constructivist art in *75HP*. Additionally, they both painted in the cubist style at the same time.

If we were to judge Iancu and Maxy's cubist art strictly based on their paintings, then we would conclude that their art is quite modernist. But, when situated in the broader context of the avant-garde magazines, their cubist-oriented art acquires an avant-garde identity. By reproducing the paintings, the magazines construct relationships between them and tension between the text and the image. As mass media, print products produced in collaboration between artists, writers, and publishing houses, the magazines challenge the ideas of painting's supremacy and purity and the artist's primacy. Just as Cubism occupies a middle space between avant-garde and modernism, so too does avant-gardists' cubist-oriented art.

---

34   *Punct*, no. 16 (March 1925).
35   *75HP*, no. 1 (October 1924).

Contimporanul: Marcel Iancu's Cubist Guitar Paintings

Despite the figurative elements in their art, Romanian avant-garde artists viewed abstraction as the most advanced development in modern art. According to the article "Note de Pictura" ("Notes on Painting") in *Contimporanul*'s issue no. 4, 1922, abstraction—"named cubism by those who mistake it (for it)"—is "the painting's liberty, of life aspects and outside signs" and "a formula of pure painting, of painting for painting."[36] "Notes on Painting" espouses a modernist agenda of unyielding abstraction. At the same time, its artwork is a mix of abstract, cubist, and expressionist artworks, particularly in its early numbers from 1922 to 1924. Iancu created many woodcut prints for *Contimporanul* of portraits representing his fellow Dada friends, including Tzara and Hans Arp; he did the same in the form of political caricatures satirizing current political figures or situations. One portrait that particularly stands out from the rest is Iancu's large woodcut of writer Ion Minulescu, which he rendered in uneven, dashing black lines that mimic heavy brushstrokes.[37] I contend that German Expressionism greatly influenced these portraits, and the rest of Iancu's woodcuts, because of the interplay of flat, black and white forms enclosed in a shallow space and the intense emotional effect these forms capture in their stark juxtaposition. Iancu's black and white woodcuts are a continuation from his Zurich Dada period. Most likely, he learned about German Expressionism before Zurich Dada from his teacher Iosif Isner.[38] It is demonstrable that Iancu practiced both Expressionism and Cubism and switched effortlessly between them. Indeed, Ioana Vlasiu points out that Iancu's paintings owed much—"in equal measure"—to Expressionism and Cubism. Iancu is "on the other side of abstraction," meaning his art is not wholly abstract because, "the rigors of geometry remain for him more of a theoretical aspiration."[39] Iancu's theoretical text "Notes on Painting," attempts to convince the magazine's readers that abstraction is the most advanced development to which artists should aspire. However,

---

36 "Note de Pictură" (Notes on Painting), *Contimporanul*, no. 4 (June 24, 1922): 13.
37 *Contimporanul*, no. 35 (March 1923).
38 A renowned Romanian artist of expressionist art in the first half of the twentieth century, Isner, who taught both Iancu and Maxy, studied at the Munich Academy of Art and published portraits and caricatures in Romanian newspapers and magazines. See *Pictori evrei din România: 1848–1948*, ed. Amelia Pavel, transl. Vivian Prager (București: Editura Hasefer, 1996), 26.
39 Ioana Vlasiu. "Idei constructiviste în arta română a anilor '20: integralismul," in *Bucharest in the 1920s–1940s: Between Avant-garde and Modernism, exhibition catalogue*, ed. Magda Cârneci (București: Editura Simetria, Uniunea arhitecților din România, 1994), 41.

when looking at the artworks in the magazine, it becomes apparent why readers might mistake abstraction for Cubism because the artworks are not entirely without figures and objects.

Take, for instance, Iancu's *Compoziție lirică* (*Lyrical Composition*) in *Contimporanul*'s issue no. 60, September 1925: a black and white photographic reproduction of one of Iancu's guitar paintings (Fig. 1). *Contimporanul*'s issues no. 61, October 1925, and no. 63, November 1925, likewise have reproductions of two more guitar paintings by Iancu. These paintings signify Cubism's impact on Iancu, particularly Picasso and Braque's cubist renderings of the guitar form. They are, however, more similar to Braque's still lifes of that period, such as *Guitar and Glass: Socrate* from 1921 and *The Mantelpiece* from 1922. Braque's still lifes are less decorative than Picasso's *Mandolin and Guitar*, which exhibits clear cut, patterned forms marked by thick lines and bright, flat colors (Fig. 2). It is quite striking that *Mandolin and Guitar* graces the front page of *Contimporanul*'s issue no. 64, March 1926. Green calls it "the most ambitious" of Picasso's paintings from 1924. *Contimporanul*'s editors incorrectly caption the painting's title and date: "*Compoziție*, 1925" ("Composition, 1925").[40] Nevertheless, the fact that the magazine published Picasso's painting within a short timespan after its creation testifies to the magazine's pursuit of new trends in Cubism. Additionally, Braque's still lifes, as in Iancu's, retain some modeling through tonal variations and painterly brushstrokes that add a layer of depth to the objects. I venture to surmise that Iancu was studying closely Braque's depictions of still life when he embarked on his cubist paintings.

---

40   *Contimporanul,* no. 64 (March 1926). Its 1924 date and its *Mandolin and Guitar* title is taken from *Pablo Picasso: A Retrospective,* edited by William Rubin (New York: The Museum of Modern Art, 1980), 196.

Fig. 1: Marcel Iancu, *Compoziție lirică* (Lyrical Composition), *Contimporanul*, IV, no. 60 (September 1925), Biblioteca Digitală a Bucureștilor (http://www.digibuc.ro/colectii/avangarda-romaneasca-c2049).

Fig. 2: Pablo Picasso, *Compoziție* (Composition), *Contimporanul*, V, no. 64 (January 1926), Biblioteca Digitală a Bucureștilor (http://www.digibuc.ro/colectii/avangarda-romaneasca-c2049).

The magazine numbers are not special numbers on Cubism, nor do they contain special features on Cubism or Picasso, other than a reproduction by Juan Gris's painting *Natura moartă* in issue no. 61, October 1925. Iancu's paintings are placed next to random poetry and prose. In issue no. 60, the large image of *Lyrical Composition* is on the cover page alongside a poem by Ion Barbu. The poem is about the fictional utopian place "Isarlâk." Iancu's *Studiu de suprafață* (*Surface Study*) resides on the upper right of a "Piano" poem and an "Erik Satie" article (Fig. 3).[41] Indeed, the text is about music, but about piano, not guitar music. It is as if the editors of *Contimporanul*, Iancu and Ion Vinea, struggled to find an artwork of a piano. The cover page of issue no. 63 has Iancu's *Decompoziție* (*Decomposition*) on the top right, next to Ion Barbu's poem "Uvedenrode" (Fig. 4).[42] The poem takes place at a fictional ravine called Uvedenrode where "many gastropods" are "super sexual/super musical" while a girl keeps

---

41 *Contimporanul*, no. 61 (October 1925).
42 The poem "Uvedenrode" is part of Ion Barbu's poetry volume *Joc secund*, 1930.

slipping on the rocks until "you," i.e., the reader, wraps her in "light creeks." [43] The poem's whimsical rhymes and its reference to music complement Iancu's guitar painting. Its end rhymes "Gasteropozi!//Mult limpezi rapsozi//Moduri de ode//Ceruri eșarfă//Antene în harfă," in which the first two lines rhyme with each other and the last two lines do the same, elicit the sound of musical gastropods singing odes under an open winter sky.[44] However, it is a stretch to assert that the editors deliberated profusely on the placement of the image.

Fig. 3: Marcel Iancu, *Studiu de suprafață* (Study of Surface), *Contimporanul* IV, no. 61 (October 1925), Biblioteca Digitală a Bucureștilor (http://www.digibuc.ro/colectii/avangar da-romaneasca-c2049).

---

43 Ion Barbu, "Uvedenrode," *Contimporanul*, no. 63 (November 1925).
44 The lines roughly translate to "Gastropods!//Very clear rhapsodists//Modes of Ode//Skies scarf/Harp antennas."

Fig. 4:   Marcel Iancu, *Decompoziție* (Decomposition), *Contimporanul*, IV, no. 63 (November 1925), Biblioteca Digitală a Bucureștilor (http://www.digibuc.ro/colectii/avangarda-romaneasca-c2049).

Instead, Iancu and Vinea detached the word and image, suggesting one did not need to rely on the other to complete each of their separate meaning; they exist independently of each other. How are we to interpret these images then, if the text and image placement barely offer any indication as to why the image appears on a certain page, in a certain magazine number? Iancu's cubist guitar paintings are not the only images that Vinea and Iancu place in this manner. The rest of the images in *Contimporanul*'s numbers, like in the other Romanian avant-garde magazines, exhibit the same detachment between word and image, except when an article features an artist and her/his art, or when Iancu's portraits illustrate a writer of a featured poem or story. Then why should we pay special attention to how Iancu's cubist paintings are reproduced in the magazine? One argument is that the separation of the image from the text enhances the significance and meaning of the image in question. The image can then be more prominent on the page because it is not tied to any particular arrangement of text, whether to confirm the text's meaning or to decorate it.

With Iancu's cubist paintings as independent images, *Contimporanul* establishes the significance of Cubism in Romania through the cubist practice of one of the most talented and prolific Romanian avant-garde artists. Iancu writes that Cubism is "the last stage in the evolution of painting from four centuries and onwards."[45] According to him, Cubism engages with "the problem of plastic construction" and "only in this moment the acknowledgment of plastic elements has been sought."[46] He goes on to describe the superiority and beauty of "plastic reality," that which the artist summons in art, over physical reality via the plastic elements of "line, color, and volume," but especially color.[47] It is difficult to grasp the brilliance of this plastic reality in the magazine's black and white reproductions. Iancu superimposed two guitar forms in *Lyrical Composition* on an abstract background. The white areas surrounding the guitars imbue them with volume. Although the composition is decipherable in the reproduction, it loses the subtlety of shades and tints, of color variations, and of texture. The triangles at the top of the composition hint at Iancu's preoccupation with Constructivism and abstraction, as in his *Relief A7* published in the Zurich Dada magazine *Dada* issue no. 1, July 1917, and in the Romanian avant-garde magazine *Punct* issue no. 5, December 1924, with the title *Construcţie de: Marcu (sic) Iancu* (Fig. 5). In *Relief A7*, Iancu constructed an abstract plastic reality out of wooden geometric parts that, when assembled, create depth on a flat surface through cast shadows.

---

45 Marcel Iancu, "Cubism," *Contimporanul*, no. 71 (December 1926): 4.
46 Ibid.
47 Ibid.

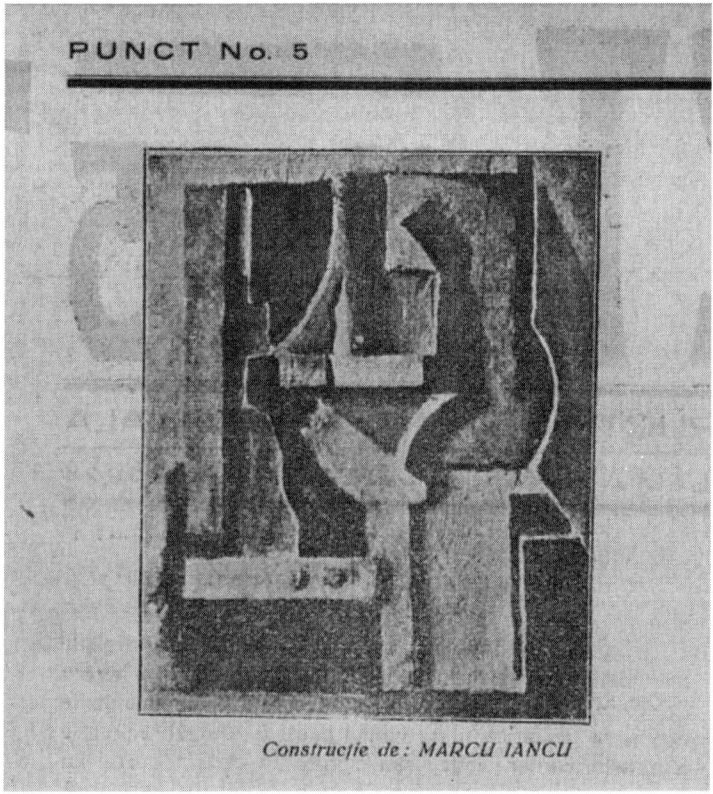

Fig. 5: Marcel Iancu, *Constructie de: Marcu (sic) Iancu* (Construction by Marcu Iancu), *Punct. Revista de artă constructivistă internațională*, no. 5 (December 20, 1924), Biblioteca Digitală a Bucureștilor (http://www.digibuc.ro/colectii/avangarda-romaneasca-c2049).

In addition to the geometric forms, *Lyrical Composition* shares with *Relief A7* a vertical composition and the build-up of depth, albeit with oil paint on canvas. In the absence of the original painting's color palette, the black and white reproduction evokes a discernible affinity with Iancu's older relief, which begs the question: why did Iancu choose to paint in the cubist manner rather than more abstractly? Perhaps Iancu veered towards Cubism because through it he could study "the problem of plastic construction"—that which Cubism explored.[48] He stopped making the type of re-

---

48   Ibid.

liefs of his Zurich Dada period after his return to Romania. In a 1982 interview, Iancu reminisces about his Zurich Dada period, stating that afterward, he "continued the idea of abstract art, intuitive and instinctive."[49] Therefore, he did not stop with abstraction upon his return to Romania. On the contrary, he experimented with constructivist architecture. His interior constructions "directly into the walls" stemmed from his Dada reliefs.[50] *Surface Study* repeats the guitar motif but its outlines are better defined than in *Lyrical Composition*. However, this may be due to the fact that the reproduction of the former is of a higher resolution than the latter. Nonetheless, Iancu's confidence seems to have grown in manipulating looser brushstrokes, building tension between overlapping forms, and moving the background forward in space.

Surface Study exemplifies a constructivist composition, but it retains referents to real objects. Mariana Vida describes the "evolution" of Iancu's art in phases, from the "violent expressionism toward tamed constructivism of the abstract forms, followed by a figurative formula, hinting at the new objectivity."[51] Perhaps the phases are not as clear cut as Vida assesses. As mentioned earlier, Iancu published expressionist portraits throughout *Contimporanul*'s lifetime, which ended in 1932. Additionally, Vida does not take into account Iancu's constructivist woodcuts, which appeared in *Contimporanul* just before his cubist paintings. Iancu's *oeuvre* indeed culminates in figurative, less abstract, work by the 1930s, but it can be argued that his work in *Contimporanul*, *Punct*, and *Integral* does not represent a linear evolution.

Issue no. 49, November 1924, of *Contimporanul* is one of the last to feature a constructivist linocut by Iancu: a diagonal composition in a machine aesthetic and red and blue colors (Fig. 6). The special *Contimporanul* issue no. 50–51 acts as an exhibition catalogue for its "First International Exhibition." The catalogue includes, among other of his work, another Iancu linocut and his cubist painting *Cabaret Voltaire* that he completed in Zurich. In later issues, the number of Iancu's constructivist artworks decreases, and, thus, justifies the hypothesis that his work evolved from abstraction to figuration. Yet, the abstract work is not "followed by a figurative

---

49 Francis M. Naumann, "Janco/Dada: Entretien Avec Marcel Janco," in *Dada, Circuit Total*, ed. Henri Béhar and Catherine Dufour (Paris; Lausanne: Éditions L'Age d'Homme, 2005), 174.
50 Ibid., 169.
51 Mariana Vida, "Marcel Janco's Graphic Art and the Metamorphoses of the Avant-Garde Language in Fine Arts," *Marcel Janco in Interwar Romania: Architect, Fine Artist, Theorist*, eds. Anca Bocanet, Dana Herbay, Nicolae Lascu et al. (București: Editura Simetria, Uniunea Arhitectilor din România; Editura Meridiane, 1996), 178.

formula" but by cubist work, classifiable as existing between figurative and abstract. *Contimporanul*'s issue no. 60 is the first time in which we encounter Iancu's work that conveys a significant cubist influence.

Fig. 6: Marcel Iancu, *Linoleum*, *Contimporanul*, III, no. 49 (November 1924), Biblioteca Digitală a Bucureștilor (http://www.digibuc.ro/colectii/avangarda-romaneasca-c2049).

Integral: M.H. Maxy's Cubist Portraits

In the article "Cronometraj-pictural" ("Pictorial Timekeeping"), published in *Contimporanul*, M.H. Maxy outlines the critical characteristics of Cubism, Dadaism, and Constructivism. He describes Dadaism as "Cubism saved," perhaps meaning that Dadaism allowed Cubism to continue its maturation during and after World War I.[52] To call "Pictorial Timekepeing" an article is inaccurate. It reads more like a visual poem or a visual history of art movements. Maxy wrote each section with different vertical and horizontal positions of words and phrases, for example, like he did with the bolded letters

---

52 M.H. Maxy, "Cronometraj-pictural" (Pictorial Timekeeping), *Contimporanul*, no. 50–51 (December 1924).

of the word "Reviziure" (Revision), which run vertically one by one in a column form in the Cubism section. This position of the word "Revision" is set against the horizontal positions of the words "light, color, and form" as though to emphasize that Cubism revised these design elements.

Cubism has a significant position in Maxy's visual history, following the "genesis of sentimentalism," with sentimentalism and ends with Constructivism.[53] Maxy insinuates that Cubism was the first movement to break from the "individualism" and the "romanticism" of sentimentalism, opening art to the radical possibilities of Dadaism and Constructivism. Cubism's characteristics are described in a column as: "conception of painting, composition, equilibrium, structure, economy, measure, synthesis."[54] With a concern for composition and synthesis, Cubism revised "light, color, and form" as these design elements no longer served the "plastic representation" and "illusion" of sentimentalism. Instead, Cubism led to Dadaism's "open road towards abstraction" and Constructivism's "death of painting."[55] Maxy's "Pictorial Timekeeping" is one prominent example of how admiration for Cubism grew in the Romanian avant-garde by means of cubist artworks and articles, referencing Cubism, that were published in the avant-garde magazines.

Contimporanul was not Maxy's singular outlet for circulating his engagement with Cubism. His magazine *Integral* was the main outlet through which he not only espoused his notion of Integralism but also displayed his integralist, cubist art. Speaking primarily about the magazine's literary output, Nicolae Bârna is of the opinion that the editors of *Integral* "did not arrive at radical innovation that they promoted in their theoretical texts" because they also published modernist writers who already enjoyed critical acclaim in the mainstream media.[56] The same can be said of the magazine's artistic output. In his 1926 painting *Construcţie Umană (Human Construction)*, Maxy represents two peasant women, monumental in size, wearing traditional folk outfits and carrying baskets on their heads while striding forward (Fig. 7). Maxy's peasant women are comparable to Braque's enormous nude woman in his classical painting *Nude Woman with Basket of Fruit* (1926) that is part of his Canephorae series.[57] *Human Construction* is also from 1926, though the magazine does not mention its date. In both paintings, the figures occupy an ambiguous

---

53 Ibid.
54 Ibid.
55 Ibid.
56 Nicolae Bârna, *Avangardismul literar românesc: studiu şi antologie* (Bucureşti: Editura Gramar, 2003), 16.
57 Karen Wilkin, *Georges Braque* (New York, London, Paris: Abbeville Press, 1991), 67.

space. The horizontal line marking the ground in *Human Construction*, similar to the dark foreground in Braque's painting, is the single element that conveys depth in the composition. It is possible that Maxy knew of Braque's work with classicism. However, Maxy's figures contain the cubist aspect of two dimensional, geometric forms, in the appearance of the massive, draping skirts and blouses. As is more evident in the original color version, the women do not recede into the darkly lit background as in Braque's painting but emerge heroically, heavily modeled with cast shadows as though they are sculpted heroines epitomizing every Romanian peasant woman. Maxy represents the peasant icon as representative of Romanian identity, and, hence, merges the cubist style with the Romanian nationalist style. The heroic and monumental peasant subject of *Human Construction* is ubiquitous in Romanian nationalist paintings of the first half of the twentieth century; for example, in the paintings of artists like Camil Ressu and Francisc Şirato.

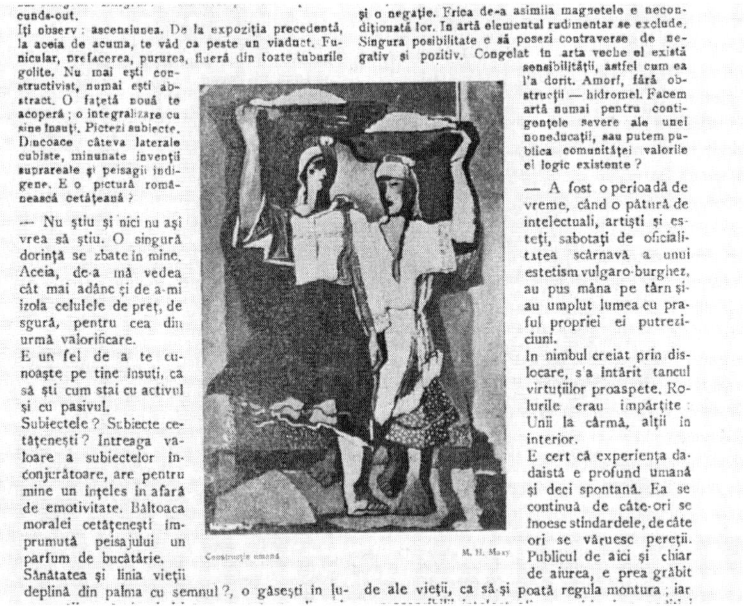
cunds-out.
Iți observ : ascensiunea. De la expoziția precedentă, la aceia de acuma, te văd ca peste un viaduct. Funicular, prefacerea, pururea, flueră din toate tuburile golite. Nu mai ești constructivist, numai ești abstract. O fațetă nouă te acoperă ; o integralizare cu sine însuți. Picterzi subiecte. Dincoace câteva laterale cubiste, minunate invenții suprareale și peisagii indigene. E o pictură românească cetățeană ?

— Nu știu și nici nu aşi vrea să știu. O singură dorință se zbate în mine. Aceia, de-a mă vedea cât mai adânc și de a-mi izola celulele de preț, de sgură, pentru cea din urmă valorificare.
E un fel de a te cunoaște pe tine însuți, ca să ști cum stai cu activul și cu pasivul.
Subiectele ? Subiecte cetățenești ? Intreaga valoare a subiectelor înconjurătoare, are pentru mine un înțeles în afară de emotivitate. Băltoaca moralei cetățenești împrumută peisajului un parfum de bucătărie.
Sănătatea și linia vieții deplină din palma cu semnul ?, o găsești în lu-

Construcție umană

M. H. Maxy

și o negație. Frica de-a asimila magnetele e necondiționată lor. In artă elementul rudimentar se exclude. Singura posibilitate e să posezi contraverse de negativ și pozitiv. Congelat în arta veche el există sensibilității, astfel cum ea l'a dorit. Amorf, fără obstrucții — hidromel. Facem artă numai pentru contigențele severe ale unei noneducații, sau putem publica comunității valorile ei logic existente ?

— A fost o perioadă de vreme, când o pătură de intelectuali, artiști și esteți, sabotați de oficialitatea scârnavă a unui estetism vulgaro-burghez, au pus mâna pe târn și-au umplut lumea cu praful propriei ei putreziciuni.
In nimbul creiat prin dislocare, s'a întărit tancul virtuților proaspete. Rolurile erau împărțite : Unii la cârmă, alții în interior.
E cert că experiența dadaistă e profund umană și deci spontană. Ea se continuă de câte-ori se înoesc stindardele, de câte ori se văruesc pereții. Publicul de aici și chiar de aiurea, e prea grăbit de ale vieții, ca să-și poată regula montura ; iar

Fig. 7: **M.H. Maxy, *Construcţie Umana* (Human Construction), *Integral: revistă de sinteză modernă*, no. 11 (February–March 1927), Biblioteca Digitală a Bucureștilor (http://www.digibuc.ro/colectii/avangarda-romaneasca-c2049).**

The National Theater in Bucharest hosted the exhibition "Bucharest in the 1920s–1940s: Between Avant-garde and Modernism" in 1993. The exhibition catalogue's editor Magda Cârneci explains that the exhibition necessitated the insertion of modernism in its title because the Romanian avant-garde, as a movement, "oscillates between avant-garde and modernism."[58] The Romanian avant-garde does not completely meet the standard definition of the avant-garde, remaining solely aesthetic, with no political involvement, and inconsistent with the revolutionary Russian avant-garde of the early twentieth-century.[59] Poignantly, "its moderate utopianism aims at best at rapid modernization, not at total transformation of the world. Its nihilism is juvenile, its anarchism is regenerative."[60] Within the context of Cârneci's critique of the Romanian avant-garde, Integralism is a modernist endeavor, for it complements the avant-garde's lackluster, "moderate utopianism" in the sense that Integralism is not a tendency meant to radicalize and reinvent art like constructivist art did. But this is what makes the Romanian avant-garde unique—its integralist tendency to join diverse art styles together without the need to denounce one, such as the cubist style, as inferior because it was supposedly out of fashion.[61] As Picasso scholar Simonetta Fraquelli has shown, Picasso's simultaneous practice in both the classical style and the cubist style was "a passionate declaration of his freedom of expression and a desire to embrace a stylistic pluralism that defied all forms of dogmatism" and a tenacious stance against those who found Cubism "obsolete."[62]

Iancu and Maxy and their avant-garde magazines defied the avant-garde call for a break with the past in favor of a continued dialogue with earlier avant-garde experimentation, such as that of Cubism. They looked back to Cubism to create new, integralist art that defined the Romanian avant-garde as a distinct, rather than forgotten or redundant, tendency among the European avant-gardes. Maxy conceived of *Integral* and its "modernism" not as "the adaptation of movement x or y but an integral

---

58 *Bucharest in the 1920s-1940s*, ed. Magda Cârneci, 1.
59 Ibid., 15.
60 Ibid., 16.
61 In the 1920s, Romanian avant-gardists embraced all avant-garde movements and styles, though some, like Ilarie Voronca, were hostile to Surrealism. Voronca, in "Surrealism and Integralism," viewed Surrealism "inferior" to Dada and Constructivism because of its "feminine expressionism" and because it "does not respond to the rhythm of the time," 5.
62 Simonetta Franquelli, "Double Play—Cubism and Neoclassicism in Picasso's Art 1914–1924," *Picasso: The Great War, Experimentation, and Change*, edited by Mariah Keller (New York, NY: Scala Arts Publishers, 2016), 17.

manifestation of the same European spirit throughout all its spread spiritually-geographically."[63] With his concept of Integralism, Maxy stressed the Romanian avant-garde's originality and distinction while at the same time clarifying that it lies in "the same modernist nuclei" that is present across Europe and in Romania too.[64] Integralism is, therefore, for him a means to absorb modernist European art styles.

Like Iancu's, Maxy's artistic career began with Expressionism, followed by Constructivism (*Punct* and *Integral* included his constructivist works) and gradually became cubist and figurative, though these stylistic categories often overlap in his art. On the cover of *Integral* no. 11, February–March 1927, Maxy juxtaposes the constructivist black and white design of the typeface with his painting *Lopătar* (*Boatman*) fitted neatly in the lower right and surrounded by white space (Fig. 8). The figure of the boatman, like the peasant women in Maxy's *Human Construction*, is gigantic, confined in a space that has no foreground or background, with fragments of a water wheel and shimmering water. The flat background mimics the boatman's flat, distorted body. Gheorghe Dinu tells Maxy during an interview published in *Integral*: "You are no longer constructivist. You are no longer abstract. A new face is covering you: an integralism with itself. You paint subjects. Here a few cubist sides, wonderful surrealist inventions and indigenous landscapes."[65] *Boatman* epitomizes one of Maxy's cubist subjects and his gradual reintroduction of the figurative in his paintings. Petre Oprea writes that Maxy's integralism deals with "subjects inspired by the lives of the lower class," and are "ethnically speaking, cubist, without giving up color."[66] This shift in Maxy's art, from constructivist to cubist, from generalized subjects to socio-politically minded ones, is apparent in the difference between his 1924 painting *Construcție Umană* (*Human Construction*) and the 1926 of the same name which is now at the National Museum of Romania in Bucharest. The two paintings do not have much in common except for their title. In the 1924 painting, Maxy painted a reclining female figure that does not signify the labor of the lower class or the peasantry. Her abstracted body of multiple spheres becomes just another geometric form among the rest.

---

63 M.H. Maxy, "Politica Plastica," *Integral*, no. 9 (December 1926): 3.
64 Ibid.
65 Gheorghe Dinu, "Initiale pentru Expozitie: De Vorba cu M.H. Maxy," *Integral*, no. 11 (February–March 1927): 5–7.
66 Petre Oprea, *M.H. Maxy* (București: Editura Meridiane, 1974), 21.

Fig. 8: M.H. Maxy, *Lopătar* (Boatman), *Integral: revistă de sinteză modernă*, no. 11 (February–March 1927), Biblioteca Digitală a Bucureștilor (http://www.digibuc.ro/colectii/avangarda-romaneasca-c2049).

Within the span of *Integral's* three-year run, 1925 to 1928, Maxy's art transitioned from constructivist, abstract compositions to cubist portraits. He also changed to a freer interpretation of Integralism that crossed beyond the boundaries of Constructivism to the experimentation with multiple styles. In his 1922 *Cetatea Modernă* (*The Modern Citadel*), published in *Integral* no. 12, April 1927, Maxy tries hard to emulate Picasso and Braque's Analytic Cubism with fragmented planes of monochromatic colors (at least in the reproduction) that fractures the city landscape into abstract forms (Fig. 9). Maxy's analytic cubist phase is also on display in his 1922 painting *Nud cu văl* (*Nude with Veil*), which was not printed in *Integral* but can be seen at the National Museum of Art of Romania. The difference between *Boatman* and *The Modern Citadel* is stark. Maxy probably detected no conflict in including both paintings in the magazine because they signified his exploration of Cubism—an essential aspect of his integralist style. Once *Integral* ended its run in 1928, Socialist Realism consumed Maxy's career throughout and post-World War II.

Fig. 9: M.H. Maxy, *Cetatea Modernă* (The Modern Citadel), 1922, *Integral: revistă de sinteză modernă*, no. 12 (April 1927), Biblioteca Digitală a Bucureștilor (http://www.digibuc.ro/colectii/avangarda-romaneasca-c2049).

Conclusion

To celebrate Romanian avant-garde art of the 1920s and 30s, Romania issued a series of stamps in 2004. Among the six stamps in the series—including the artists Merica Ramniceanu, Jean David, Marcel Iancu, Victor Brauner, M.H. Maxy, and Hans Mattis-Teutsch—Iancu and Maxy's stamps are the only ones to feature cubist art. Iancu's painting *Compoziție (Composition)*, 1926, as titled on the stamp, and Maxy's portrait *Tristan Tzara,* 1924, epitomize the substantial influence that Cubism had on both artists' artistic practice, given that these stamps aim to display the art that best identifies each artist (Fig. 10) (Fig. 11).[67] Maxy's cubist portrait of Tzara appeared in *Contimporanul* issue no. 50–51, November–December 1924, but Iancu's *Composition* of a seated female figure did not appear in *Contimporanul* nor *Integral*. Nevertheless, both paintings attest to Iancu and Maxy's productive mid-1920s period in which they ardently pursued their cubist painting practice that would solidify their status as foremost artists of the Romanian avant-garde. The two artists stopped their cubist practice by 1930 as the Romanian avant-garde waned in a country that would soon push Jewish artists, like Iancu and Maxy, into exile within or outside Romania. For a future study, it would be worthwhile to determine to what extent cubist art in the Romanian avant-garde magazines influenced a younger generation of Romanian artists who worked during the Communist years and may have produced their own version of cubist art as they looked back to the avant-garde for an artistic and political alternative to Socialist Realism.

---

67 For example, the painting *Femeia care visează II* (*Woman who dreams II*), 1934, on Brauner's stamp is a painting in his quintessential surrealist style for which he is most known in the studies of avant-garde and modern art.

Fig. 11: M.H. Maxy, *Tristan Tzara*, 1924, stamp, 2004 (https://commons.wikimedia.org/wiki/File:Stamps_of_Romania_2004-108.jpg).

Fig. 10: Marcel Iancu, *Compoziție, 1926* (Composition, 1926), stamp, 1924 (https://commons.wikimedia.org/wiki/File:Stamps_of_Romania_2004-111.jpg).

The Romanian Judicial Professions Database: An Open-Source Tool for Researching the Romanian Legal System

Radu Pârvulescu

Abstract: *Justice is a perennial topic in scholarship on Romania, from socialist legality, through transitional justice, and to anti-corruption studies. Systematic study of law and justice has been stymied, however, by lack of basic information: who was doing what, where, when, and how? To begin to address this shortcoming, this brief article introduces the Romanian Judicial Professions Database, a new, open-source tool which provides yearly, individual data on 10,000 judges, 6000 lawyers, 5500 prosecutors, 3000 notaries public (notari publici), and 1000 bailiffs (executori judecătorești), in some cases going back to the 1970s. The database can be downloaded at https://osf.io/gfjke/ and supporting software is available at https://github.com/r-parvulescu/ro_judicial_professions.*

> "Astăzi, avem acces la monografii despre orașe și sate, despre instituții cu importanță limitată, dar despre justiție încă nu. / Today, we have access to monographs on cities and villages, on institutions of limited importance, but not yet on justice"
>
> —Iuliu Crăcană, *Dreptul în slujba puterii: justiția în regimul comunist din România, 1944–1958/Law in the Service of Power* (București, Romania: Institutul Național pentru Studiul Totalitarismului, 2015), 20.

Introduction

Law and justice are arguably the most studied elements of contemporary Romania, often as they relate to personnel issues. Researchers have questioned, did Ceaușescu-era magistrates dominate transitional justice? How many judges retired early due to incessant fights over anti-corruption? Are all public notaries (*notari publici*) appointed based on nepotism? Such questions have been difficult to answer because data on Romanian legal professionals are secret, scattered, or both. This article introduces the Romanian Legal Professions Database, a new, open-source directory with yearly, person-level data on 10,000 judges, 6,000 lawyers, 5,500 prosecutors, 3,000 notaries public (*notari publici*), and 1,000 bailiffs (*executori judecătorești*). These new data allow us to investigate, over many years and in great detail, aspects of the Romanian legal system that have puzzled and eluded previous researchers.

My aim in this brief article is to introduce a new research "product" to scholars of Romanian justice. I therefore focus on the basics: what the database contains and how it was put together. I conclude by highlighting strengths and weaknesses of the Romanian Judicial Professions Database, and by showing how the open-source nature of the dataset makes it easy for researchers to both use and contribute to these data.

Scope of the Romanian Judicial Professions Database

The Romanian Legal Professions Database is a product of the author's dissertation research on the evolution of Romanian legal professions from 1978 to 2018. In essence, the database is a yearly record of practicing judges, prosecutors, lawyers, notaries public, or bailiffs.[1] A legal professional is "practicing" when they are in good standing with their professional association and/or the Ministry of Justice and consequently have the right to judge cases, defend clients in court, draw up contracts, etc.[2] The data coverage of each profession varies. Appendix A describes the temporal and geographic coverage of the pre-2005 magistrate sample. Nationally complete, yearly censuses are also available for notaries from 1995 to 2019, and for bailiffs from 2001 to 2019. Finally, the database covers full-right lawyers (*avocați definitivi*) in the Bucharest bar, by far the largest bar in the country, for the years 2001, 2002, 2005, and 2006.[3] Table 1 summarizes the scope of the database.

---

1 This database does not include information on court clerks (*grefieri*) or jurisconsults (*juriști*), the latter who are in-house legal consultants in both the public and private sectors. Clerks have their own national professional organization, postgraduate clerk school, career ladder, and pension system, while jurisconsults are not professionally organized and are paid, promoted, etc. according to the norms of their employer, though one must be a law school graduate to legally bear the title of "*jurist.*"
2 That said, each year features a handful of professionals that are, for any number of reasons, in the profession but not entitled to practice, typically because they are under investigation for malpractice.
3 That is, lawyers who have successfully passed their two-year apprenticeship, or *stagiu*.

Profession/Group	Years Available	Approximate Count of Unique Individuals	Notes
Judges	1978–2020	10,000	Sample 1978–2004, complete population after 2005
Lawyers	2001, 2002, 2005, 2006	6,000	Bucharest bar only
Prosecutors	1988–2020	5,500	Sample 1978–2004, complete population after 2005
Notaries Public *(notari publici)*	1995–2019	3,000	Compete population
Bailiffs *(executori judecătorești)*	2001, 2003–2019	1,000	Complete population
Law School Graduates	1974–2019	NA	Aggregate data: 1974–2019 for U.B.B. Cluj, 1986–2019 for A.I. Cuza Iași

Table 1: Summary of data availability for five judicial professions and one extra-professional group (law school graduates)

These data are organized as tables of "person-years," where each row contains information on a particular person in a particular year. Tables 2 and 3 exemplify such person-years, one for a judge and the other for a notary. As can be seen, certain basic information is always available: unique person ID, surname, given name, sex/gender and geographic area. Other information varies by profession: only for bailiffs and lawyers do we have the street address of their offices, for example. Appendix B lists the information available for each profession.

Person ID	Surname	Given Name	Sex	Work place	Year	Appeals Code	Tribunal Code	Low Court Code	Level
2291	Corbu	Alina Corina	F	Trib-unalul Bucu-rești	2006	CA4	TB9	NA	2
2291	Corbu	Alina Corina	F	Curtea de Apel Bucu-rești	2007	CA4	NA	NA	3

Table 2: Example of person-year entry for a judge.

Person ID	Surnames	Given Names	Sex	Year	Chamber	Town
2921	Toader	Tudorel	M	2018	Iași	Iași
2921	Toader	Tudorel	M	2019	Iași	Iași

Table 3: Example of person-year entry for a notary public.

Finally, the database also includes aggregate information on graduates from two of Romania's "traditional" faculties of law, those of Babeș-Bolyai University in Cluj-Napoca (U.B.B. Cluj) and Alexandru Ioan Cuza University in Iași (A.I. Cuza Iași). To be exact, the database includes the total number of graduates for each year between 1974 and 2019, broken down by sex/gender. These figures give an indication of the size and gender composition of the labor supply of legal experts over this period, since as a rule one must be a law school graduate to practice in these legal professions.[4]

Data Sources

The largest part of the Romanian Judicial Professions Database comes from online, publicly available membership rolls published by the National Union of Romanian Bailiffs and the Superior Council of the Magistracy, the latter being the joint professional body of judges and prosecutors.[5] Data on public notaries and lawyers were voluntarily shared with the author after submitting written requests to the National Union of Notaries Public of Romania and the Bucharest bar.[6] To access pre-2005 information on judges and prosecutors the author filed freedom of information requests (per law 544/2001) with courts and prosecutor's offices, soliciting the names of magistrates on their payrolls (*state de plată*) for the years 1978–2004. Aggregate data on law school graduates were likewise obtained from via freedom of information requests to U.B.B. Cluj and A.I. Cuza Iași.

All told the author has collected several thousand membership and pay rolls: automated data processing is therefore a necessity. This is achieved using an original software package written by the author in the Python programming language, and freely available at https://github.com/r-parvulescu/ro_judicial_professions. The software automates routine tasks: centralizing information from separate files into one table, standardizing diacritics, and so on. That said, one particular type of

---

4   Through the whole period under study there have been various "back doors" through which one could enter the legal professions, which often involved previous tenure as a legal expert or jurisconsult in the state apparatus. Preliminary investigations indicate that such "lateral" entries, while politically and symbolically important, were in fact quite rare (figures available from the author).
5   UNEJR, *Uniunea Națională a Executorilor Judecătorești din România*; CSM, *Consiliul Superior al Magistraturii*.
6   UNNPR, *Uniunea Națională a Notarilor Publici din România*; *Baroul București*.

automated coding is non-obvious and consequential: identifying unique individuals.

The problem is that one person may have multiple names, due to inconsistent and error-prone bookkeeping or caused by real name changes, for example upon marriage. Table 4 illustrates both the name-diversity problem and my solution. While by default a computer assumes that the names in the left-hand column refer to six different people, a human would immediately recognize that all these names point to a single individual. The most complicated part of the software is therefore dedicated to name standardization, that is, to transforming the names in the left-hand column to the single, unitary name in the right-hand column.[7] Once the names are standardized the software assigns unique IDs to each distinct name, while ensuring that people with identical names (usually common ones like "Ioan Pop") are not spuriously combined. The documentation on the previously-mentioned GitHub site provides technical details.

Year	Raw Name	Standardized Name
2007	Marcela Sandu	Marcela Viorica Popescu Sandu
2008	Marcela Sandu	Marcela Viorica Popescu Sandu
2009	Marcela Viorica Sandu	Marcela Viorica Popescu Sandu
2010	Marcela Viorica Sandu-Popescu	Marcela Viorica Popescu Sandu
2011	Marcela Sandu-Popescu	Marcela Viorica Popescu Sandu
2012	Marcela Sandu-Popescu	Marcela Viorica Popescu Sandu
2013	Marcela Popescu	Marcela Viorica Popescu Sandu
2014	Marcela Viorica Popescu	Marcela Viorica Popescu Sandu
2015	Marcela Viorica Popescu	Marcela Viorica Popescu Sandu

Table 4:   Illustration of name transformation by the name standardizing software.

Strengths, Weaknesses, and the Power of Open Source

The first strength of the Romanian Judicial Professions Database is its scope, as it features extensive temporal coverage and person-level entries (including names) on five judicial professions. Second, the database is both free and easy to use, as the work of collecting and cleaning the data has already been done. Finally, the database is transparent: when in

---

[7] The name standardiser also puts given names and surnames in alphabetical order, to preclude the possibility that "Marcela Viorica Sandu" and "Viorica Marcela Sandu" would be considered as two different people.

doubt, anyone can consult both the "raw" data sources and the code that processes them.[8]

As of this writing, the principal weaknesses of the Romanian Judicial Professions Database is the lack of person-level information, limited to name, gender, location, and career information, such as the year in which a person retired. This database therefore lacks the richness of historical and survey studies: for example, we do not know whether a legal professional was a Communist Party member, how they viewed their work, or whether they were married. The Romanian Judicial Professions Database trades depth for breadth. The second shortcoming is the database's patchy but ever-improving coverage. Existing gaps are partly due to a minority of chief magistrates refusing freedom of information requests addressed to their institution. Worse, however, is lax archiving. The National Union of Romanian Bars, for instance, updates daily an online list of all practicing Romanian lawyers but never saves versions of that list, so a digital archive never accumulates.

In lieu of a conclusion, I would like to highlight the "open source" nature of the Romanian Judicial Professions Database, which allows anyone to take the data and use them as he or she sees fit, provided that he or she cite this article. "Open source" also allows researchers to contribute to the database, for example by adding professional membership rolls that will be released in the future, or historical payrolls obtained from their own freedom of information requests. Moreover, they can modify the companion software, for instance by using the newest machine-learning algorithms to perfect name standardization and unique person identification. Finally, they can link the Romanian Judicial Professions Database to other sources of information, such as the yearly wealth declarations (*declarații de avere*) which all magistrates must submit, or case information from particular trials. It is my hope that tools like the Romanian Judicial Professions Database will usher in a new wave of research on justice in Romania.

Appendix A: Counties Sampled for Pre-2005 Magistrate Employment Rolls

Note that counties (*județe*) with courts of appeals (e.g. Timiș) only feature data on appellate judges and prosecutors after 1993, when the appellate level was reintroduced in Romania. As of the September 2020, the sampled counties and their available years are:

---

[8] Both the "raw" data and the processed, person-year tables are available at https://osf.io/gfjke/, while the software can be found at https://github.com/r-parvulescu/ro_judicial_professions.

Judges

The High Court of Cassation and Justice (1988–2004), Bistrița (1978–2004), Maramureș (1878–2004), Sălaj (1988–2004), Galați (1975, 1985–2004), Brăila (1988–2004), Vrancea (1988–2004), Iași (1978–2004), Vaslui (1979–2004), Satu Mare (1989–2004), Bihor (2000–2004), Buzău (1978–2004), Dâmbovița (1978–2004), Prahova (1978–2004), Mureș (1978–2004), Harghita (1978–2005), Caraș-Severin (1978–2004), Arad (1978–2004), Timiș (1988–2004), Bacău (1988–2004), Neamț (1978–2004), Dolj (1978–2004), Gorj (1978–2004), Mehedinți (1978–2004), Olt (1979–2004), Argeș (1978–2004), Tulcea (1978–2004), Alba (1978–2004), Hunedoara (1978–2004), Sibiu (1978–2004), Suceava (1980–2004), Botoșani (1988–2004), Teleorman (1978–2004), Călărași (1981–2004), Ialomită (1978–2004).

Prosecutors

Suceava (1995–2004), Botoșani (1978–1988, 1995–2004), Giurgiu (1978–2004), Ialomița (1978–2004), Călărași (1981–2004), București (1988–2004), Dâmbovița (1988–2004), Vâlcea (1988–2004), Olt (1978–2004), Mehedinți (1988–2004), Sibiu (1978–2004), Brașov (1994–2004), Covasna (1978–2004), Mureș (2001–2004), Harghita (1978–2004), Bacău (1988–2004), Neamț (1978–2004), Vaslui (1988–2004), Sălaj (1978–2004), Bistrița (1988–2004), Maramureș (1978–2004), Satu Mare (1978–2004).

Appendix B: Attributes/Variables by Group

Judges

Unique person ID, surnames, given names, sex/gender, workplace, year, appeals area code, tribunal code, low court code, judicial level.

Lawyers

Unique person ID, surnames, given names, sex/gender, year, office address, office type (solo, small office, joint offices, legal corporation), trial level at in which can plead (low court, appeals, all courts)

Prosecutors

Unique person ID, surnames, given names, sex/gender, workplace, year, appeals area code, tribunal code, low court code, judicial level.

Notaries Public (*notari publici*)

Unique person ID, surnames, given names, sex/gender, year, chamber, town, inheritor status.

Bailiffs (executori judecătoreşti)

Unique person ID, surnames, given names, sex/gender, office address, year, chamber, town, apprenticeship (*stagiu*), inheritor status, non-categories ("other") information

Law School Graduates (aggregate data)

Number of female graduates, number of male graduates

Reviews

Constantin Iordachi. Liberalism, Constitutional Nationalism, and Minorities: The Making of Romanian Citizenship, c. 1750–1918. Leiden: Brill, 2019. 682 pp.

Review by Mara Mărginean,
George Barițiu Institute of History, Cluj-Napoca, Romania

Most of the time, historians of modern Europe discuss the birth of nation-states through the lenses of the Western processes of modernization, cataloging the evolution of Eastern European, African, or South American territories as illustrations of deficient modernity at large. In his extensive and thoroughly documented book *Liberalism, Constitutional Nationalism, and Minorities: The Making of Romanian Citizenship, c. 1750–1918*, Constantin Iordachi proposes a welcome departure from this model. Through "a socio-intellectual history of the politics of citizenship" (p. 21) during the long 19th century, Iordachi highlights the process of consolidation of the Romanian state as an excellent illustration of alternative modernization.

Studies on Romania's modern history have examined the national leaders' involvement in the international negotiations between the Great Powers, as well as the domestic social and cultural stakes of such actions. These contributions are important because they shed light on various facets of the Romanian elites' emancipation and Westernization during the second half of the nineteenth century. But Iordachi's approach advances our knowledge from at least two points of view. First, it brings the Phanariot and Russian experiments into the historiographical conversation analyzing Romania's nation-building. He argues that taking a *longue durée* approach would flesh out "patterns of continuity and ruptures between the Old Regime (*ancien régime*) and the New Regime of the modern nation-state" (p. XIII), which may be relevant to a better comprehension of nineteenth-century global social and economic transformations. Second, it highlights the making of national institutions of citizenship as entanglements between Western models of governance and local practices. Because of these encounters, however, approaches to citizenship not only enhanced the making of an "educated, socially emancipated and motivated by patriotic values" (p. XIV) modern citizen but also led to restrictions, sometimes even exclusions, of minority groups from the right to citizenship. Ultimately, Iordachi makes a case for looking at citizenship from the angle of how the census system was given meaning through successive readings of concepts such as gender, ethnicity, or migration.

The first part of the book, "From the Old Regime to the Nation-State: Toward a Unified Moldo-Wallachian Citizenship, c. 1750–1858," consists of four chapters. Iordachi looks at how the financial and political pressures of the Ottoman Empire forced the oligarchy of the two principalities to articulate political and land rights for the population born or naturalized in those territories. He then assesses the successive reinterpretations of these legislative regulations during the period between the Organic Regulations and the Revolution of 1848. Although ethnic aspects weighted less in the eighteenth-century approaches to citizenship, already by the early nineteenth century non-permanent citizens and ethnoreligious minorities were gradually excluded from civil rights. Furthermore, Iordachi discusses the abolition of Roma slavery in 1855/1856. While pointing out the increasing restrictions imposed upon foreigners at the time, he argues that the emancipation agenda of the local elites was part of a liberal transnational movement to mobilize civil society for citizen inclusion worldwide. These mechanisms of interconnection between local dynamics of civil society and global changes in the meaning of citizenship are used in the last chapter of this section to detail the European premises of the unification of the two principalities in 1859.

The second part of the book, "Peasants into Romanians: The Construction of Romanian National Citizenship, 1859–1866," consists of two chapters. Analyzing in tandem the attempts of Moldova and Wallachia to regulate citizenship, Iordachi highlights the similarities and differences between the two in implementing civil rights, especially the right to own land. He goes on and shows how divergent views on citizenship turned into tensed political confrontations after 1859. The book makes a plea for reading the process of administrative centralization and marginalization of the Moldovan elite through the lenses of citizenship policies. It links the exacerbation of anti-Semitic feelings in Moldova to the actions of the political elite in Bucharest in the context of the unification of the two principalities.

The last part of the book, "Constitutional Nationalism and Minorities, 1866–1918," consists of additional seven chapters. It looks at the establishment of a regime of constitutional nationalism, which allowed the liberal elite to combine populism with enlightened despotism and promote an ethnonational approach to citizenship. This was made possible by bureaucratic discrimination and selective citizenship mechanisms: naturalization conditions imposed by the legislature, admission to conditional citizenship by parliament, exclusion of non-Christians from the right to own land in Romania, or denying the right to land ownership to women marrying foreign nationals. These regulations have paradoxical outcomes. On the one hand, the emancipation of native women was addressed in a much more advanced key than in most Western countries; on the other hand, the forced implementation of illiberal practices led to the segregation of Jews, which raised the attention of the international community in late nineteenth century.

Taken as a whole, Iordachi's book on the practice of citizenship is an important work that researchers concerned with legislation as a means of social regulation cannot afford to ignore. It also provides a solid starting point for further analysis of state-building processes in the modern period. I would especially welcome an approach that follows more closely the interconnections between the intellectual agenda described in detail here and the economic shifts of the nineteenth century.

Sabrina P. Ramet. Interwar East Central Europe, 1918–1941: The Failure of Democracy-building, the Fate of Minorities. New York: Routledge, 2020. 331 pp.

Review by Francesco Magno, University of Trento, Italy

Forty-six years after Joseph Rothschild's seminal work *East Central Europe between Two World Wars* (1974), a new synthesis on the interwar era in East Central Europe has been published by Routledge. Author and editor Sabrina P. Ramet has assembled an excellent team of scholars for this monograph to take on the analysis of an era that, in many aspects, bears a striking resemblance to our current world.

The appearance of a new volume on interwar East Central Europe has been extremely well received by scholars and researchers, as the last significant contribution of this kind—Ivan Berend's book, *Decades of Crisis*—was published in 2001. This multi-authored addition to the literature includes an introductory piece by Ramet and original works of international historiography examining seven countries: Poland, Czechoslovakia, Romania, Bulgaria, Albania, Hungary, and the Kingdom of Serbs, Croats and Slovenes. Each country is the focus of a specific chapter written by a scholar fluent in the country's language as well as history. The final section, written by Robert Bideleux, analyzes the peasant parties and their role in the political history of East Central Europe in the interwar period.

As suggested by the sub-title, the volume's primary focus is the failure of the region's democratization process during the interwar era. According to Ramet, the three primary causes of failed democracy-building in the area were domestic issues, the effects of the 1929 economic crises, and the rise of Nazi Germany (p. 1). Ramet breaks down the domestic issues further to include the lack of consensus on the issue of parliamentary rule, the low levels of literacy among the populace, and, above all, inter-ethnic tensions. Indeed, ethnic minorities are another common theme within the book; the weak integration of minorities within the region's nation-states and the discriminatory measures implemented by governments at the time heavily contribute to the adverse judgment of those examining this piece of history.

The afterword, written by Stefano Bianchini, provides a comparative and transnational summary to assist readers with understanding the similarities and differences among East Central European countries of the era. According to Bianchini, all the nation-states under scrutiny opted for what he calls a "minimalist approach to democracy," which consisted largely of the implementation of free and relatively fair elections while more substantial democratic procedures—such as respect for civil and social rights, the defense of minority rights, and high levels of political competition—were neglected (p. 320).

These aspects emerge clearly in the chapter about Romania, written by Roland Clark. Clark's analysis also includes analyses of other fundamental issues—including the tensions among the provinces annexed after the First World War and the relationship between nationalism and Orthodox Christianity—to provide a complete picture of interwar Romania. Furthermore, Clark deserves credit for nuancing and problematizing this twenty-year span which Romanian historiography has often described as the nation's golden age. As he correctly points out, in the interwar period, "Romania failed to develop a democratic political culture that the majority of citizens believed in and wanted to succeed" (p. 167). This holds true partially for Czechoslovakia as well. In their chapter, Ramet and co-author Carol Skalnik Leff dismantle the myth of the thriving Czechoslovak democracy by highlighting its limits on the integration of Hungarian and German minorities within the new statehood. Again, the authors deconstruct a narrative particularly popular in modern Czech society—that the First Republic represents one of the greatest political achievements of the modern age—and even the legend of Tomas Masaryk is diminished. Ramet and Leff point out that despite his undoubted merits in creating the Czechoslovak state, "he was relatively indifferent and even, at times, hostile to institution-building" (p. 83), and he heavily counted on extra-institutional methods to build up and secure his power.

The book's considerable attention to exploring the limits of democratization and the fate of minorities overshadows the positive aspects and accomplishments of the interwar period in East Central Europe. While it is fair to acknowledge failures and limitations that affected progress in the area, the general development of this era in which the countries of the region tried to fill the cultural, political and economic gap with the West by engaging in an all-encompassing process of modernization should not be underestimated. If more space could have been found to include the remarkable achievements of this era, this volume would provide a more complete narrative of the 1920s and 30s in East Central Europe. However, as written, this book presents reliable and updated analyses that are useful for experienced scholars looking for transnational and comparative perspectives and students approaching the subject for the first time.

Dorina Roșca. Le grand tournant de la société moldave. "Intellectuels" et capital social dans la transformation post-socialiste. Paris: Presses de l'Inalco, 2019, 359 pp.

Review by Petru Negură, Humboldt Fellow, Leibniz Institute for East and Southeast European Studies, Regensburg, Germany

Dorina Roșca's book is a study of the sociology of intellectuals in the Republic of Moldova during the late socialist era and the period of "systemic transformation" that began with *perestroika*. The research relies on qualitative data (21 in-depth interviews with respondends employed in different areas of Moldova during the late Soviet time) and quantitative data (128 responses to a questionnaire survey, with a non-probabilistic sample and analyzed through descriptive statistical analysis) conducted by the author in 2007–2008. Throughout the book, the author explores the hypothesis that social capital (political and relational) played an important role in the emergence, socio-economic survival, and socio-professional re-conversion of Moldovan intellectuals, before and after 1991.

The definition of social capital theorized by Pierre Bourdieu, Mark Granovetter, Nan Lin and others emphasizes the relational dimension by which a person's status consists of the number and quality of his/her social relations. In Bourdieu's elaboration, social capital is in a relationship of interdependence with other types of capital—economic, cultural, and symbolic. Especially in the socialist and post-socialist context, the institutional relations of an individual were of particular significance. These relations reflect, in the Soviet context, the social capital of a political type. Concurrently, the size and quality of social capital are consistent with structural inequalities between groups and individuals. One of the strong arguments of Roșca's book is that the social capital accumulated, used, and exchanged by Moldovan intellectuals during and after the Soviet period is the social element that ensures continuity between the Soviet period and the period of post-socialist "transition."

Roșca's work focuses on intellectuals, a particular social group defined and formed by two key elements: the university diploma and non-manual professional activity. In the Soviet sense of the term, intellectuals (*intelligentsia*) are non-manual employees of two types of organizations: commercial organizations (administrators, accountants, etc.) and non-commercial organizations (doctors, teachers, librarians, etc.). To these can be added a cross-cutting dimension, i.e. the administrative functions.

To highlight the meaning of the term intellectual in the Soviet context, the author, an associate researcher at the Université de Paris, distinguishes it from the definition of the intellectual that originated in late 19th-century France. In the context of the "Dreyfus affair," for example, the intellectual asserts himself/herself as a symbolic authority in opposition to power. In contrast to this definition, the Soviet intellectual is not at all an agent of autonomy but a constituent element of the reigning power and the "ideological state apparatus," to use the concept coined by L. Althusser. Although explainable, the quotation marks added to the (Soviet) term of intellectual thoughout Roșca's book introduce a polemical note and a normative position, according to which the (authentic) intellectual would by definition be autonomous from any center of of power. An "archaeological" foray into the idea and mission of intellectuals in the communist thought by the Austro-Marxist thinkers and other Marxists like R. Luxemburg, A. Gramsci, V. Lenin—would have been perhaps more enlightening in the context of the history of intellectuals in Eastern Europe and in Russia.

Roșca's book is also a study of economic sociology, in the spirit of and based on the concepts of Karl Polanyi and Mark Granovetter, according to whom economic processes are inseparable from social evolutions. The author argues for the importance of social capital in a "shortage economy" (Janos Kornai) and for a "principle of reciprocity" based on horizontal solidarity ties (K. Polanyi). Further, in line with the works of Alena Ledeneva and others, the book analyzes relationships of informal support in socialism and post-socialism. Furthermore, it considers the social support network as a central element for Moldovan intellectuals not only in their tactics of socio-economic survival but also in their strategies of socio-professional reconversion moving from the late Soviet period to the post-1991 "transformation".

One of the remarkable contributions of the book lies in its exploration of the historical dimension that contextualizes and gives meaning to the researched object. Thus, the book investigates the large-scale social processes influenced by the political transformations during the "traditional" communist period (1940–1985) and "reformist" socialism (1985–1991), such as the exodus of intellectuals in 1940 and 1944, the mass education system, the evolution of the literacy and schooling rates and the trends of structural social mobility. Certain cultural peculiarities are also examined, such as the evolution of the proportion of ethnolinguistic groups within the administrative elites. The book observes, for example, that there were high numbers of administrators of all ranks of "alien" origin, compared to "natives" ones. Here we note *en passant* that the reader may sometimes get the impression of a form of theoretical ethnicization. The author appears to give the ethnic factor a disproportionate relevance, which overshadows the social factors themselves. Differences in ethnic distribution often hide social categories, as Roșca explains very well, reflected by the shortage of specialists at all levels, especially in rural areas with low literacy. Moreover, the author's use of categories such as "native" and "allogeneic," are not without ambiguity. Bessarabia was not ethnically homogeneous before 1940 nor after. The data produced by the Soviet state—a political regime that ethnicized social groups—should therefore be considered with discernment.

The book addresses the contradictions and aporias of Soviet ideological discourse regarding the classless society, studying the genesis and way of life of the "new" class of intellectuals, in addition to the workers and peasants class, considered dominant. The increase in the number and proportion of intellectuals from 9.8% in 1959 to 22.8% in 1985 shows the importance given to this group in the Soviet system. The devaluation of intellectuals in post-1990 "Moldovan capitalism" is evidence of the social and human regression marked by the post-socialist period, against the background of endemic economic crises, drastic decline in public spending on social welfare, the bankruptcy of enterprises, destruction of cultural institutions and, not least, the separation of Transnistria that the author calls "economic amputation."

The systemic transformation started during the *perestroika* years and continued in the early 1990s, determined Moldova's intellectuals to adopt more or less successful accommodation strategies through re-professionalization and/or migration. Even though the in-depth interviews illustrate the suffering and humiliation accompanying the massive process of downward social mobility after the fall of the USSR, they also highlight successful cases of socio-economic adjustment thanks to previously acquired social capital and willingness to embrace the new ideological *doxa* (ethnic nationalism and a liberal economic doctrine).

The post-socialist transformation is theoretically reframed and critically re-examined by Roșca, thus, contrasting the numerous studies of normative and teleological "transitology." The book retraces the directions of "transition," discussed in the early 1990s by the renewed political class of Moldova, divided between "conservatives" and "reformers" and symbolically dominated in 1990–1991 by the latter, i.e. the representatives of the Moldovan Popular Front and the reformist wing of the Communist Party. The Moldovan decision-makers' poor implementation of the three processes imposed by the "Washington consensus" (liberalization, privatization, stabilization) led to drastic poverty and socio-professional turmoil. To intellectuals, the many NGOs created and financed by international organizations in the field of education, culture, and human rights constituted both a lifeline and a way of socio-professional and ideological re-conversion during the post-socialist "systemic transformation."

In the end, Roşca's analyses, historically contextualized within a rich theoretical corpus, capture the historical dynamics and biographical substance of large-scale transformation processes that took place in the Republic of Moldova, and may be similar to those in other post-socialist countries and regions.

Contributors

Roland Clark: Roland Clark is a Senior Lecturer in Modern European History at the University of Liverpool, a Senior Fellow with the Centre for Analysis of the Radical Right, and President of the Society for Romanian Studies (SRS). His first book, Holy Legionary Youth: Fascist Activism in Interwar Romania (Cornell University Press, 2015), won the SRS Book Prize in 2015 and was translated into Romanian as part of the SRS/Polirom Book Series. His second book, Sectarianism and Renewal in 1920s Romania: The Limits of Orthodoxy and Nation-Building is forthcoming with Bloomsbury in 2021. Clark researches and writes on antisemitism, fascism, the Holocaust, lived religion, theology, nationalism, and gender.
E-mail: Roland.Clark@liverpool.ac.uk

Lavinia Stan: Lavinia Stan is Professor in the Department of Political Science at St. Francis Xavier University, Canada. A Comparative Politics specialist, she has written extensively on religion and politics, transitional justice, and post-communist democratization. She is the co-author or co-editor of *Religion and Politics in Post-Communist Romania* (Oxford University Press, 2007), *Transitional Justice in Post-Communist Romania: The Politics of Memory* (Cambridge University Press, 2013), and *Post-Communist Romania at 25: Linking Past, Present and Future* (Rowman & Littlefield, 2015), among others. Stan was Vice-President and then President of the Society of Romanian Studies from 2010 to 2018, currently serving as Past President.
E-mail: lstan@stfx.ca

Lucian Turescu: Dr. Lucian Turcescu is Professor, Graduate Program Director, and past Chair the Department of Theological Studies at Concordia University, Montreal, Canada. He has done research, published, and taught in several areas, including early Christianity, religion and politics, and ecumenism. Some of his books include (co-edited with L. Stan) *Justice, Memory and Redress in Romania* (2017), (co-authored with L. Stan) *Church, State, and Democracy in Expanding Europe* (2011); *Religion and Politics in Post-communist Romania* (2007); (co-edited with L. DiTommaso) *The Reception and Interpretation of the Bible in Late Antiquity* (2008); and single-authored *Gregory of Nyssa and the Concept of Divine Persons* (2005). He has also authored over 50 peer-reviewed articles.
E-mail: Lucian.Turcescu@concordia.ca

Valeska Bopp-Filimonov: Valeska Bopp-Filimonov studied Cultural Studies at Leipzig University, with a focus on Romania and other Eastern and Southeastern European countries. She completed her PhD in History in 2012 with a thesis on the relationship between public and private accounts of the socialist period in Romania. To do this, she analyzed biographical interviews using a mixed-methods approach combining sociological approaches, historical research and discourse analyses. Since 2017, she works at the Institute of Romance Studies at Friedrich Schiller University Jena. She teaches courses for students of Romance and Southeastern European Studies. Her current research topics are perspectives on socialism and the transformation period in contemporary Romanian literature, Romanian childhood(s) in literature and film, and the history of Romanian Studies in the German speaking countries (Germany, Austria, Switzerland).

E-mail: valeska.bopp-filimonov@uni-jena.de

Amelia Miholca: Amelia Miholca is an American-Romanian artist and art historian, currently a PhD student at Arizona State University. She holds an M.A. in Art History and B.A.F. in Painting, both also from Arizona State University. Her specialization is the avant-garde and modernism, with an interest in Eastern European, post-socialist and post-colonial art.

E-mail: Amelia.Miholca@asu.edu

Radu Pârvulescu: Radu Andrei Pârvulescu is a doctoral candidate in the Department of Sociology at Cornell University, and a visiting scholar in the Department of Sociology, Anthropology, and Social Work at the University of Dayton. His interests include legal systems, the sociology of professions, stratification, social theory, and quantitative methods.

E-mail: rap348@cornell.edu

EAST EUROPEAN STUDIES: JOURNALS AND BOOK SERIES

Soviet and Post-Soviet Politics and Society

Editor: Andreas Umland

Founded in 2004 and refereed since 2007, SPPS makes available affordable English-, German-, and Russian-language studies on the history of the countries of the former Soviet bloc from the late Tsarist period to today. It publishes between 5 and 20 volumes per year and focuses on issues in transitions to and from democracy such as economic crisis, identity formation, civil society development, and constitutional reform in CEE and the NIS. SPPS also aims to highlight so far understudied themes in East European studies such as right-wing radicalism, religious life, higher education, or human rights protection.

Journal of Soviet and Post-Soviet Politics and Society

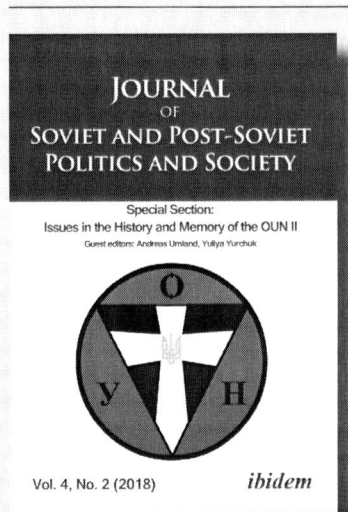

Editor: Julie Fedor

The Journal of Soviet and Post-Soviet Politics and Society was launched in April 2015 as a bi-annual companion journal to the Soviet and Post-Soviet Politics and Society book series (founded in 2004 and edited by Andreas Umland, Dr. phil., Ph.D.). Like the book series, the journal provides an interdisciplinary forum for original research on the Soviet and post-Soviet world. The journal strives to publish creative, intelligent, and lively writing, which tackles and illuminates significant issues and is capable of engaging wider educated audiences beyond the academy.

UKRAINIAN VOICES

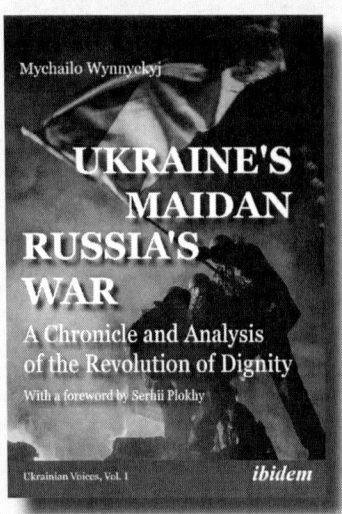

Editor: Andreas Umland

The book series "Ukrainian Voices" publishes English- and German-language monographs, edited volumes, document collections and anthologies of articles authored and composed by Ukrainian politicians, intellectuals, activists, officials, researchers, entrepreneurs, artists, and diplomats. The series' aim is to introduce Western and other audiences to Ukrainian explorations and interpretations of historic and current domestic as well as international affairs. The series was founded in 2019, and the volumes are collected by Andreas Umland, Dr. phil. (FU Berlin), Ph. D. (Cambridge), Senior Research Fellow at the Institute for Euro-Atlantic Cooperation in Kyiv.

FORUM FÜR OSTEUROPÄISCHE IDEEN- UND ZEITGESCHICHTE

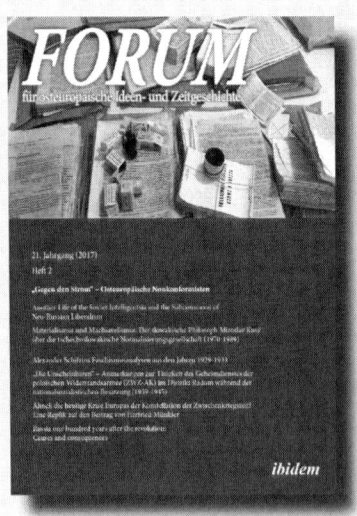

Editors: Leonid Luks, Gunter Dehnert, Alexei Rybakow, Andreas Umland

FORUM is a bi-annual journal featuring interdisciplinary discussions on the history of ideas. It showcases studies by political scientists, philosophers as well as literary, legal, and economic scholars, and books reviews on Central and Eastern European history. The journal offers critical insight into scientific discourses across Eastern Europe to Western readers by translating and publishing articles by Russian, Polish, and Czech researchers.

ibidem Press | Leuschnerstr. 40 | 30457 Hannover | Germany
Phone: +49 (0) 511 2 62 22 00 | Fax: +49 (0) 511 2 62 22 00 | sales@ibidem.eu

Literature and Culture in Central and Eastern Europe

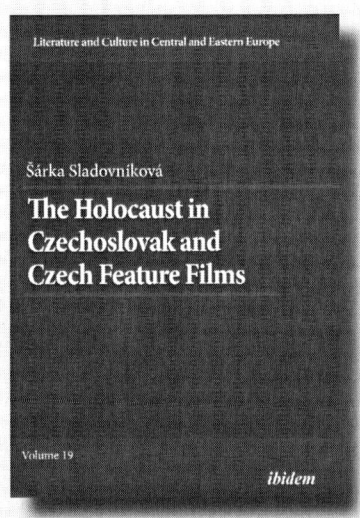

Editor: Reinhard Ibler

The book series Literature and Culture in Middle and Eastern Europe aims to provide a forum for current research on literature and culture in Central and Eastern Europe. It prioritizes a spatial-regional concept over a purely philological one, e.g. Slavic, in order to better reflect the numerous interrelationships that characterize the literature and cultures of Eastern Central, Southeastern and Eastern Europe as well as the German-speaking world. The series aims to uncover these manifold mutual contacts, overlaps, and influences, both individually and as a whole.

In Statu Nascendi

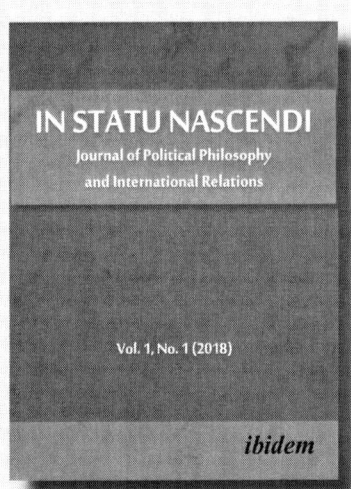

Editor: Piotr Pietrzak

In Statu Nascendi is a peer-reviewed journal aspiring to provide a world-class scholarly platform, which encompasses original academic research dedicated to the circle of Political Philosophy, Cultural Studies, Theory of International Relations, Foreign Policy, and the political Decision-making process. The journal investigates specific issues through a socio-cultural, philosophical, and anthropological approach to raise a new type of civic awareness about the complexity of contemporary crises, instabilities, and warfare situations, where the eponymous "stage-of-becoming" plays a vital role.

www.ibidem.eu | facebook.com/ibidem.Verlag

ibidem

ibidem.eu